L

Wildlife Congregations

A Priest's Year of
Gaggles, Colonies,
and Murders by
the Salish Sea

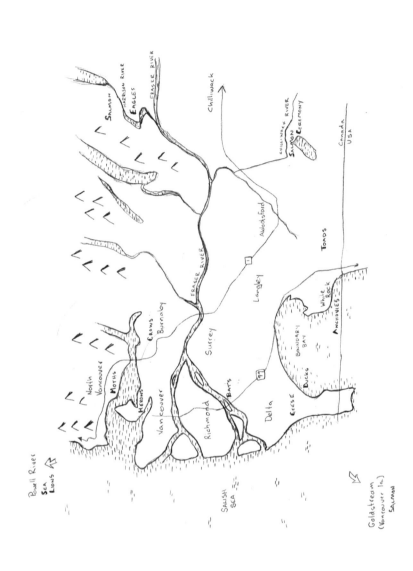

If you talk to the animals they will talk with you and you will know each other. If you do not talk to them you will not know them, and what you do not know you will fear. What one fears one destroys.

— Chief Dan George, Tsleil-Waututh Nation

hancock
house

Printed in South Korea

FRONT COVER DESIGN J. RADE
PRODUCTION & DESIGN by J. Rade, M. Lamont
EDITING BY D. MARTENS

Hancock House gratefully acknowledges the Halkomelem Speaking Peoples whose unceded, shared and asserted traditional territories our offices reside upon.

We acknowledge the support of the Government of Canada through the Canada Book Fund and the Canada Council for the Arts, and of the Province of British Columbia through the British Columbia Arts Council and the Book Publishing Tax Credit.

Canada

Published simultaneously in Canada and the United States by
HANCOCK HOUSE PUBLISHERS LTD.
19313 Zero Avenue, Surrey, B.C. Canada V3Z 9R9
#104-4550 Birch Bay-Lynden Rd, Blaine, WA, U.S.A. 98230-9436
(800) 938-1114 Fax (800) 983-2262
www.hancockhouse.com info@hancockhouse.com

CONTENTS

ACKNOWLEDGEMENTS

The first and most essential acknowledgement is that this book was written on and about unceded Coast Salish Territory: land, geological formations, and waters that have been in reciprocal relationships of care with xʷməθkʷəy̓əm (Musqueam), Skwxwú7mesh (Squamish), and səlilwətaɬ (Tsleil-Waututh) people, and with living beings like Salmon and Cedar from time immemorial. As a settler, my personal and familial love of and relationship with this place is relatively new, and is only possible because of an ongoing genocidal colonial project that included displacement, active and passive germ warfare, incarceration, child removal, destruction of culture and language, and outright murder. No acknowledgement or apology can change that reality. In an effort towards accountability to both land and people I try and often fail to amplify the work and voices of Indigenous people, to support and compensate Indigenous workers and projects, and to take action in solidarity, particularly in struggles to protect Indigenous peoples' relationships and obligations to this territory. Indigenous collaborators and contributors to this project have consented to the use of their work and have been compensated in ways and amounts that they consider appropriate. I also acknowledge that there are Indigenous stories, songs, technologies, and practices that belong only to Indigenous communities and peoples and are not mine to share.

Next, I acknowledge with gratitude the community of readers and editors: Melanie Delva, Erin Flegg, Kate Foran, Tim Nafziger, Eddie Sloane, Bruce Triggs, Christine Thuring, Lydia Wylie-Kellerman, consulting librarian Keith Bunnell, and especially Sarah Shepherd, who enthusiastically read and edited almost the entire first draft.

Thank you to those who read chapters about their experiences: Denzil Asche, Agnes Pedersen, and Myriam Dykstra, who, although she would prefer that no one ever use the word, pointed out that 19 was far too many times for the word flesh to appear in one chapter, even in a chapter about sea lions; Ron and Laura Berezan, who laughed in the right places and encouraged me to think more about how large numbers of creatures impact large numbers of humans. Others who appear by name—Jeff Calvert, Caitlin Beck—thanks for sharing these adventures. And thanks as well to those who trusted without reading that what I wrote would not besmirch their reputations: Cameron Gutjahr, Lini Hutchings, and Jason Wood.

Thank you to all those who shared their expertise. Conservationist Ian Barnett reviewed the goose and duck chapters and clued me in to the importance of the North American Waterfowl Management Plan. Ornithologist Robert Butler checked the crow and heron chapters for accuracy. Lindsay Dealy, who works on eulachon, lamprey, and rockfish at the Department of Fisheries and Oceans, directed me to a relevant study on anchovies. Eddie Gardner, tireless Wild Salmon defender, took time to share and explain aspects of Sto:lo knowledge and culture. Rowenna Gryba read the chapter on sea lions and gently schooled me on the things that marine mammal people "just don't say." Christy Juteau, Conservation Science Director at A Rocha Canada, reviewed the chapter on toads. Myles Lamont checked the chapter on Bald Eagles. Maria Morlin, friend of the Stanley Park herons, read the heron chapter. Billie Pierre and Audrey Siegl vetted my territorial acknowledgment. Master beekeeper Andrew Scott read the chapter on moths and caught my error on antennae. Artist Ted Lyddon Hatten shared ideas, enthusiasms, and the term "ornith-theology." Environmental assessment specialist Jessica Steele connected me to other readers and to resources on marine life for enthusiasts of all ages. Luke Warkentin, of the Salmon Watershed Lab, taught me about salmon pee. Robyn Worcester, metro Vancouver Natural Resource Management Specialist, reviewed the chapter on bats. Any errors in biology and ecology are my own; my Bachelor of Science degree is old and I reside firmly in the camp of the amateurs.

I am grateful to those whose work, writing, and thinking undergirds and scaffolds this project: Ched Myers, longtime articulator and champion of watershed discipleship and watershed literacy for Christians; Brooke Jarvis, whose *New York Times Magazine* article "The Insect Apocalypse Is Here" sparked many of the ideas in the book; and Pinar and So Sinopoulos-Lloyd, founders of a little grassroots organization called Queer Nature, whose brilliant, thoughtful, and integrity-filled work on race, power, indigeneity, and nature is a touchstone for me.

Books seldom conform to their authors' imaginings, and that is also worth acknowledging. My year of immersion in animal aggregations did not happen the way that I supposed it would. I didn't witness the herring spawn or the subsequent feeding of Brant Geese. I spent very little time with the vast numbers of migrating shorebirds that feed at Roberts Bank. I saw Trumpeter Swans in fields from the car window, but I never got any closer. Further afield, I was not whistled at by hundreds of Yellow-Bellied Marmots, although I spotted a few as I floated down the Thompson River on an inflatable "party boat" full of teenagers at summer camp. Despite my ardent desire, I never made it to the admittedly almost inaccessible Tufted Puffin breeding colony on Triangle Island, north of Vancouver Island. And, although this would definitely have been cheating, I did not travel to the Narcisse Snake Dens north of Winnipeg to see 10,000 Red-Sided Garter Snakes emerge from hibernation.

A note about the names of creatures: the convention in written English is that the common group and species names for animals and plants do not begin with a capital letter unless they include the name of a person or place, like the Townsend's big-eared bat or the California sea lion. Yet we capitalize human family names, countries, languages, political parties, religions, and religious denominations. The recent and needed linguistic shifts to capitalize Black and Indigenous demonstrate that capitalization is an indicator of value and personhood. Therefore, following the examples of Potawatomi botanist

Robin Wall Kimmerer, author of *Gathering Moss* and *Braiding Sweetgrass*, and Vancouver Island nature writer Briony Penn, I have capitalized the names of plant and animal families, species, and well-known populations. I have also used capitalization in some Indigenous contexts where there is a kin-relationship between a person or people and a particular animal or entity. Marine mammal biologists do not refer to the large black-and-white toothed whales as orca unless using their Latin binomial *Ornicus orca*, but I follow the popular local habit of avoiding the term *killer whales*, since they are not technically whales, nor are they a threat to humans.

I also refer quite regularly to the Divine, the Sacred, Mystery, and occasionally to God. These are terms I use mostly interchangeably.

A note about racism and sexism in environmentalism and conservation: This book includes epigraphs from the Bible, western literature, and folk traditions and references to the work of conservationists, naturalists, and scientists. My intention in including these is to connect to the places where my own white and Christian heritage expresses love for and relationship with the more-than-human world, to evoke the wonder experienced by those who witnessed and recorded some of the now-lost animal abundance of this continent, and to highlight and amplify the work of women naturalists. None of these things are simple.

Much of the historic European and North American settler discourse around nature and conservation is rife with sexism and even more with racism. Settlers expressing wonder at abundance were often also documenting its destruction. John Muir, the progenitor of the American National Parks system, promoted the eradication of Ahwahnechee tribal members to preserve the "pristine wilderness" of Yosemite. Audubon Society movement founders like Mary Thatcher and Minna Hall promoted wild bird conservation by exploiting tropes of women's vanity and promoting a class-linked ideal of femininity. Abolitionist and naturalist Thoreau's Walden sojourn famously included bringing his laundry home to mother. Laura Ingalls Wilder's *Little House* books are filled with appreciative detail about plant and animal life, but they also romanticize "wild Indians" while simultaneously documenting her family's part in the illegal occupation, displacement, and starvation of the Osage people in Montgomery County, Kansas. Gene Stratton Porter was captivated and awed by the forest, while idealizing the lumber barons who cut it down. Theodore Geisel, who lampooned industrial destruction of ecosystems under his pen name Dr. Seuss, enjoined young readers to "speak for the trees" and to care "a whole awful lot," and he also performed in blackface as a student and in the 1920s, '30s, and '40s produced blatantly racist cartoons. Each of these sources is in the public domain, or the portions excerpted are of a length and proportion that fall under the fair dealing provision of Canadian copyright law. I made this decision in order to direct funds away from the holdings of white individuals and families and towards artists and thinkers who are Black, Indigenous, and people of colour.

This fraught heritage is part of the ongoing reality of any conservation, ecological, or environmental effort. In our own time, eco-fascism is on the rise; its combination of environmentalism, gender essentialism, northern European nature religions, and far-right politics has roots in Nazi ideology. As a white environmentalist, I try to combat this rise by being honest about and vigilant against the ways that I have been steeped in these ideas. I do not suppose that my own writing can be free from the pervasive culture of white supremacy, but I hope with accountability partners and allies to continue in the ongoing work that Maya Angelou called doing "the best you can until you know better, and when you know better, do better." I also include these roots and forebears because I am wary of the alternative—white people who want to distance ourselves from the harms of our traditions and histories can end up cut off from our roots and seek to appropriate or graft ourselves onto other (often Indigenous) peoples' traditions. We can end up uncritically idealizing Indigenous people, or, in the case of those who are doing contemplative ecology or spiritual work in nature, we can act as though we have discovered something when we are actually new arrivals to practices that Indigenous and other racialized people have engaged in for centuries.

A note about references: At the end of each chapter are "Sources and Resources," a lightly annotated list of books, articles, websites, and organizations. Some of these are citations, the places where I learned the information that I have shared, others are resources to help readers learn more. To try to balance the preponderance of white voices at the beginning of chapters, I have tried to include contributions by Indigenous knowledge-keepers and scientists and conservationists from racialized communities. Some readers will spend time with only one creature or chapter, so there are resources and references that appear at the end of multiple chapters.

Sometimes wilderness and outdoor recreation areas can be zones of exclusion, places that are not accessible because you need a car, or special equipment, there are entrance fees, you have to be away overnight, because wilderness places have been unsafe for people in your community, or you don't see other people who look like you in those places. Most of the creature-encounters in this book are fairly accessible: none required expensive equipment, and most were in transit-accessible public parks during daylight hours. I am grateful for the work of Judith Kasiama, founder of Colour the Trails, and Melissa Hafting of the BC Young Birders Program to make outdoor spaces more racially inclusive.

Although it will be read mostly by adults, I first experienced the kind of love and wonder for creatures that I hope this book engenders as a child, and I think that kind of awe can be transmitted intergenerationally. I imagine parents, grandparents, other-mothers, guncles, and other beloved adults reading aloud choice quotes to younger family members, exploring resources together, and most importantly encountering the creatures themselves. To that end, the "Sources and Resources" section for each chapter includes picture books and novels, as well as field guides and websites. I would be remiss if I did not thank Cookie Silveria and Isaac and Cedar Wylie-Fahey, who shared their animal book recommendations with me and who I imagined listening to some of these stories as I wrote them.

Thanks to Jana Rade for the cover art, for your patience with all the changes, and your flexibility in incorporating some of my images. All chapter photographs were taken by me, with the exception of the Hemlock Looper Moth by Raisa Mawji, the Lesser Snow Geese by Kath Biebrich and the Northern Anchovies by Erin Flegg. The comparison of bat, bird, pterosaur wings is by Teach 2 Imagine.

I am grateful to my family—Harriet, Myriam, Julie, and Bruce—and to my church community, Salal + Cedar, for their patience, encouragement, and support.

My greatest gratitude is to the creatures: the murders and colonies, gaggles and shoals that let me come near.

WILDLIFE CONGREGATIONS

Down By the River

Preface

I went down to the river to pray,
Studying about that good old way,
And who will wear the starry crown,
Oh Lord, show me the way.
Oh children, let's go down,
Come on down, don't you want to go down?
Oh children, let's go down.
Down to the river to pray.

Black Church Traditional

On the first day of January I found myself standing among a group of mostly strangers on the bank of the Chilliwack River. About 50 of us balanced unsteadily on the smooth river rocks, earlier than most of us seemed ready for, a little puffy-faced and blurry-eyed as an icy wind cut down the course of the water.

There was no mass gathering of any one species, unless I counted my own, and after driving east through the 2.5-million human sprawl of the Vancouver metropolitan area I was well aware that 50 is not so many of us. But I had decided to spend a year getting close to local animals in large numbers, and this gathering seemed the right place to start, or as some Coast Salish people say, "to set my intention."

The smell of wood smoke drifted through the small crowd. Everyone had dressed to stay warm and walk safely over uneven ground, but otherwise the fashion was as varied as the participants: camouflage, button blankets, leopard print, woven Cedar bark, expensive recreational gear, Cowichan sweaters, down jackets, Salish-weave wool headbands, polar fleece, and well-used work clothes. Toques were by far the most common items, and drums. At least 30 hand drums—hide stretched over wooden frames—as small as a salad plates and as large as truck tires, some the natural colour of the skins, others painted with Eagle, Bear, Orca, Frog, Salmon, feathers, trees, and water. Many people were Indigenous, but judging from faces (though that's not always the way to tell), we were a group with ancestors from all the major land masses—North and South America, Asia, Africa—as well as that troubled cluster of peninsulae on the northeast edge of the Asian continent: Europe. Across the river an adult Bald Eagle sat high in a tree, seemingly indifferent to our presence.

I could see a few people I knew: a family from Langley, a poet and professor from Emily Carr University, toddlers and grandparents, one of the Kwekwecnewtxw Watch House Keepers, Indigenous elders who protect and monitor the route of the proposed Trans Mountain Expansion Project from a Cedar house in Burnaby. It was no surprise that the greatest number of familiar faces were from rallies and demonstrations, particularly those concerned with threats to the local wild salmon populations. The ceremony was co-led by Eddie Gardner, a Sto:lo elder from the Skwah First Nation who has organized tirelessly over the past decade to raise awareness about the importance of salmon and threats to their survival like commercial overfishing and rising water temperatures, but mostly the disease, parasites, and feedlot waste from open-net fish farms.

In a Cedar bark hat, face paint made from ochre clay and animal fat, and a dark velvet shirt fringed with rows of tiny canoe paddles, Eddie stood near the fire, quietly issuing directions while warming an enormous drum painted with four salmon. On two black folding chairs, the kind that grace any church hall, was a wooden bier about a metre long, painted with a black and red salmon and covered with Cedar boughs. On top of the boughs lay the head, tail, spine, heart, and skin of a salmon. Still stiff with frost and creased from the plastic bag in the freezer, the carefully saved half-fish was frozen as though caught in the middle of a thrashing leap out of the water, vivid red flesh and glassy eye.

The Potlatch, or winter feast tradition is considered by most Sto:lo and other coastal people to be their exclusive cultural property. The ceremony at the river was neither ancient, nor secret. What we were doing that morning, a ceremony that Eddie and Gracie Kelly of the Soowhalie First Nation began sharing eleven years ago, is an assertion of sovereignty, part of a movement to revive the Halq'eméylem language and culture, and the invitation to attend had been extended broadly. Nevertheless, as a guest, a white person, and particularly as a Christian priest, the details are not mine to share.

It is enough to say that this ceremony honors the relationship between Salmon, Cedar, and Water and that those of us who gathered did so in order to humbly dedicate ourselves to caring for these three entities as our relatives. Humility is key. We were reminded by Eddie that the water, the fish, and the trees are the ones that sustain life, the ones that care for us, and that humans, in fact, have very little to offer. We heard the story of Salmon Boy, who carelessly ignored his mother's instructions to return fish bones to the water; we learned about the consequences for his people and for the Salmon People of this failure to attend to responsibility and relationship, and we learned about the incredible generosity with which the Salmon welcomed and taught the one who had harmed them. There was singing, drumming, witnessing: gifts were offered to individuals and beings. Everyone present had the opportunity to quietly set their own intentions and to take strength and encouragement to keep those commitments, both from the gathered community and from the Salmon, Water, and Cedar themselves.

Salmon, Cedar, and Water, whom Eddie called our relatives, are powerful and interconnected manifestations of life in this bioregion.

It is impossible to overstate the importance of salmon to this place. Salmon are the keystone species of coastal and rainforest ecosystems. In spring, juvenile salmon swim out to sea, where they grow, eat, and become food for larger fish and marine mammals like California Sea Lions and Orca. When adult salmon return to spawn each fall, predators and scavengers gather in estuaries and along rivers to feast. The end of the salmon life cycle delivers an annual influx of ocean-derived nutrients to the rainforest, which has even changed the chemical make-up of the trees. Salmon are central to the diet, livelihood, and culture of First Nations on the coast and inland. Salmon fishing for industry, tourism, and recreation are vital to the non-Indigenous West Coast economy and identity.

Cedar, a fragrant, versatile giant, is called "long-life giver" in some West Coast First Nations' traditions because it supplies an incredible diversity of objects and implements for daily life—clothing, blankets, diapers, ocean-going canoes, totem poles, vast Big House structures, baskets, nets, and ropes for whaling harpoons. For European settlers, harvest of the Western Red Cedar has been an economic engine of this region. Resonances between the role and symbol of the biblical Cedars of Lebanon and the local Western Red Cedar gave rise to the name of my own church community, Salal + Cedar. In contrast to the towering Cedar, Salal is a tenacious, deciduous berry bush that stays green all year.

Water, existing in three phases of matter in the tiny temperature window on this planet, is what makes the life we know possible. Water makes up 60 percent of our bodies and 73 percent of our hearts and brains; even our bones are one-third water. It is home to the Salmon, sustenance to the Cedar, and for me, water flows through the Christian story in baptism, creation, liberation, and a host of wilderness prophets like Miriam, Elijah, and John the Baptist, who heard God's call for justice beside wells and seas and rivers. A number of us gathered by the Chilliwack River had been galvanized by direct experience and media images of one of the largest social movements of the decade. When the Dakota Access Pipeline threatened the waters of the Missouri River, the thousands-strong Dakota-led resistance camps at Standing Rock faced attack dogs, water cannons, rubber bullets, and tear gas to compellingly articulate what Indigenous people around the world have known for millennia: *Mni Wiconi*—Water is Life.

The Life-Water of this place is the Fraser River. Starting in the Rocky Mountains, the Fraser is 1375 kilometres long, drains a 220,000-square-kilometre area, and pours 3,550 cubic metres of water, nearly one and a half Olympic-sized swimming pools, per *second* into the Salish Sea. The Salish Sea is the marine ecosystem that includes the straits, sounds, channels, and waterways between the Olympic Peninsula, Vancouver Island, and the mainland of British Columbia and Washington State. There is no river in the world home to more salmon than the Fraser. In the Halq'eméylem language of the Coast Salish peoples, Sto:lo means "river," and Sto:lo is the umbrella term that mainland Halq'eméylem speakers—the many interconnected Fraser River tribal groups—call themselves. The Chilliwack River, which originates in Washington State, is one of hundreds of tributaries of the Fraser. The name Chilliwack comes from the Halq'eméylem word *Tcil'Qe'uk*, which means "valley of many streams"—apt, given that the Chilliwack itself has more than a dozen tributaries.

The Chilliwack, also called the Vedder to the northwest, is known for runs of each of the five kinds of British Columbia salmon: Chinook, Coho, Chum, Pink, and Sockeye. By January, the salmon had already spawned, but Steelhead, trout that resemble salmon in behavior and size, were in the river. Clad in chest waders and hunters' camouflage, their pickups in the parking lot, Steelhead fishers were the other group at the river's edge. Perhaps only the particularly dedicated had come out to fish on New Year's morning, but they seemed completely focused on the river, content to quietly co-exist, mildly curious at most, about the ragtag party of drummers and singers sharing the riverbank.

Our location was far from private. A scramble down the bank carved by the river at its widest made the site a bit of a challenge for those who walk with canes, but we were just off a recreational trail system sponsored by the local Rotary Club. Seniors walked in pairs, families with small children drifted along the path with new bicycles and strollers, dogs walked their humans, and New Year's resolution-keepers strode along the shared equestrian trail in stretchy pants, side-stepping what my father used to call "road apples."

Earlier in the day, unsure of where we were to meet, I found my way from the parking lot by following a group carrying hand drums, stalking strangers seemed much preferable to speaking to them. I caught up with the group as they stopped in the middle of the path, looking up. About 10 metres high, in a broad, bare deciduous tree, was a Bald Eagle, blinking down at us over sharp claws. Knowing that we were arriving with a spiritual intent and that we desired access to the river, passing under the eagle felt a bit like a test. The raptor studied us, shifted to one leg and flexed a bright yellow talon, as down below we exchanged uneasy glances. It made no threatening or aggressive moves, but we all felt a tension in being so intensely observed by a predator.

I have a clergy colleague who is always nervous when I enthuse about raptors overhead. When she was a child, her older brother would point out perching hawks and eagles as they walked to the country store for candy, saying, "You see that big one up there? Now, I'm too big for it to carry away, but a little kid like you? Well …"

Back at the riverbank ceremony, participants approached the water one by one, passing by an eagle staff planted upright at the water's edge. Flight feathers blew in the wind above bright bands of color, and at the top of the staff a single talon stretched open, sharp claws curved against the sky. The drums went silent, and over the rushing water we heard the fire pop and snap behind us, and a gentle clacking as the hundred tiny paddles on

Eddie's shirt knocked together. Then, loud over these background sounds, came a fluting, piping whistle. The eagle from across the river was circling over us, calling, and after a pause, the sentry on the path responded. The two called back and forth, their thin cries in the air over our prayers.

Later, when we walked back to our cars in small groups, the eagle along the path had flown, but I noticed a shape in the tangled red and grey branches below and skidded down the rocky bank for a closer look. It was the carcass of a small hawk, suspended upside down, stark and beautiful like the hanged man in the Tarot deck. I couldn't tell if it was a Cooper's or a Sharp-shinned Hawk—these long-tailed, short-winged forest hunters are similar enough in appearance that university and museum collections sometimes need to be reclassified, so I don't hold myself to too high a standard. I wondered—was it killed by an eagle, a pellet gun, did it get caught in a snarl of discarded fishing line and become tangled in the trees?

Alive, the hawk would have been a dark slate colour on the back, with a rusty, streaked breast, but this tangle of bones and feathers was pale grey, bled of almost all color. One talon hung low and disarticulated, held together by strips of scaly skin and tendon; I could see light between the leg and foot bones, the talon curled in like a dead spider. It was a kind of visual echo of the staff by the water and the eagle in the tree. One year later, as I write this account of an era of extinction, I don't know whether it was a threat or a promise.

SOURCES AND RESOURCES

The Cedar Tree, The Heart of Our People

By Celestine Aleck
Strong Nations Publishing, 2016
An illustrated children's book about the importance of the Western Red
Cedar to Coast Salish people.

Colour the Trails

A collective of Black, Indigenous, People of Colour and Lesbian, Gay,
Bisexual, Trans, Queer and Two Spirit people in lower mainland British
Columbia, working for inclusive representation in outdoor spaces and
providing opportunities for excluded communities to participate in outdoor
recreation.
colourthetrails.com

Food Plants of Coastal First Peoples

By Nancy Turner
Royal British Columbia Museum Publications, 1995
This accessible photo-illustrated guide used in middle school curricula was
created by British Columbia's preeminent ethnobotanist in collaboration
with Indigenous knowledge-keepers.

My Heart Soars

By Chief Dan George, illustrated by Helmut Hirnschall
Hancock House, 1979
A collection of poetic essays and speeches by Tsleil-Waututh hereditary
chief, actor, and orator convey love and kinship toward plants, waters,
and creatures of his traditional territory and a sense of urgency and grief
over their destruction.

Plants of Coastal British Columbia: Including Washington, Oregon and Alaska

By Jim Pojar and Andy McKinnon
Lone Pine Publishing, 2016
The most recent edition of an accessible field guide, including photographs, illustrations and range-maps featuring nearly 800 species.

A Sto:lo – Coast Salish Historical Atlas

Edited by Keith Thor Karlson
Douglas & McIntyre, 2001
A huge and meticulous 15,000-year cultural and geographic history of the Sto:lo peoples, organized around beautifully illustrated maps.

Young Water Protectors: A Story about Standing Rock

By Aslan Tudor and Kelly Tudor
Eaglespeaker Publishing, 2018
This account of life at the Standing Rock resistance camp, where the Dakota Access Pipeline was to cross Sioux territory, was written for kids by 10-year-old Aslan Tudor of the Lipan Apache Tribe, about his own experiences. It is illustrated with photographs and maps.

WILDLIFE CONGREGATIONS

Terms of Venery

An Introduction

The Creator would appear as endowed with a passion for stars, on the one hand, and for beetles on the other, for the simple reason that there are nearly 300,000 species of beetle known, and perhaps more, as compared with somewhat less than 9,000 species of birds and a little over 10,000 species of mammals. Beetles are actually more numerous than the species of any other insect order. That kind of thing is characteristic of nature.

J. B. S. Haldane, 1947

When I discovered a few years ago that the Aberdeen Bestiary had been digitized and was available online, I immediately began to pelt my friends with choice excerpts from this 12th century illuminated catalogue of animal species that was once owned by King Henry VIII.

Some say that weasels conceive through the ear and give birth through the mouth; others say, on the contrary, that they conceive through the mouth and give birth through the ear; it is said, also, that they are skilled in healing, so that if by chance their young are killed, and their parents succeed in finding them, they can bring their offspring back to life.

Deer are the enemies of snakes; when they feel weighed down with weakness, they draw snakes from their holes with the breath of their noses and, overcoming the fatal nature of their venom, eat them and are restored.

The bear is said to get its name because the female shapes her new-born cub with her mouth, *ore*, giving it, so to speak, its beginning, *orsus*. For it is said that they produce a shapeless fetus and that a piece of flesh is born. The mother forms the parts of the body by licking it.

The underlying conviction of the Bestiary is that the whole of creation, and in particular living creatures, are revelations of the Sacred, or God if you prefer that language. It is a conviction that I unreservedly share. Inspired by this and other ancient species directories, I began to imagine writing a modern, local Bestiary, cataloguing scientific and spiritual wisdom about the creatures I encounter near my home in the lower mainland of British Columbia, where the Fraser River meets the Salish Sea. Who would not be edified by knowing that Anna's Hummingbirds glue their nests together with spider webs and Sea Otters hide favorite stones in their armpits? Who could fail to be spiritually uplifted by the resurrection story of Chum Salmon returning to spawn in a city stream after a hundred-year absence?

The floral analogue to the Bestiary is the Herbal, an illustrated volume for the identification and medicinal use of plants. Over the past decade, in certain quarters, these have had something of a revival. *The Hunger Games'* Katniss Everdeen adds edible plants to her mother's medicinal Herbal. In my social circles, white hippies and witches, Coast

Salish knowledge-keepers, and graduates of programs for "youth at risk" all carry these precious volumes about, adding notes and illustrations and pressing plant samples between rain-warped pages. The Bestiary however, has seen no parallel resurgence.

Composed in medieval monasteries, these often anecdotal, sometimes allegorical, animal encyclopedias contained the height of scientific learning. Perhaps such dubious "facts" as weasel reproduction and the snake-charming breath of deer dissuade modern would-be champions of the genre, or perhaps it is the derivative, moralizing fables.

> The flying-fish, which could not keep up with the ship, represents those who at the start apply themselves to good works, but do not afterwards persevere with them and yield to all sorts of vice, which carry them, like the restless waves of the sea, down to hell.

> The vulture feeds on the corpses of the dead as a sinner delights in the carnal desires which bring about death.

I however, was undeterred.

I am the priest of a tiny Anglican church, which gathers to break bread and say ancient prayers outdoors—under 100-year-old Western Red Cedars, beside salmon streams, on urban beaches, or along the proposed route of a pipeline to transport tar sands bitumen to the coast. Every week, I enjoin my gathered congregation to "go out on the land, listening for the Divine word, in scripture and in nature." Pastoring this little community is a braiding together of many aspects of my self and my life up to this point: love of nature, grassroots organizing and activism, and a fierce orientation to the Sacred.

Pastoring a community that prays outdoors and participating in our common work—a summer camp for youth, a creekside habitat conservation project, direct actions with Tsleil-Waututh and other First Nations opposing the expansion of the Trans Mountain Pipeline—provides a very real antidote to my own feelings of helplessness, rage, and despair as we face the catastrophic impacts of human-caused climate change and species extinctions. Not so much because I am convinced of the importance and efficacy of these admittedly modest actions, but because when I am actively engaged in these projects with my community, I do not have the capacity to be simultaneously despairing. Maybe it's just that I'm not very good at multi-tasking and these deliberate, relational acts require focused attention, akin to the kind of single-minded attentiveness I fall into when observing the living world.

As a child on Vancouver Island, I spent many backyard hours and low-budget family camping trips watching and observing: columns of ants, the shape and colour of rocks, faces suggested by the intersecting branches of trees or the grain of wood, clouds, leaves, feathers, tiny grey jumping spiders indistinguishable from concrete until they moved. The seeming monoculture of our back lawn revealed a riotous diversity: feathery white-gold seed heads; fat wide blades that make a whistle when pressed between the thumbs; ordinary blades of grass, creased down the centre, hard green at the top and tender yellow below; clover with stems sour to eat, triple leaves, and flower-heads made up of a hundred tiny orchid-like flowers; daisies pink and white with a domed yellow centre; dandelions with jagged leaves, yellow flowers, hollow stemmed seed-heads bleeding bitter white milk; buttercups full of tiny insects; and patches of moss like lush evergreen forests with tiny brown fish-hooks springing up.

As a kid with limited social skills and an almost complete incomprehension of schoolyard social hierarchy and intrigue, I found in these observations a kind of effortless connection that eluded me in interactions with my peers. Lying on my belly in the grass, or with my cheek pressed into the bark of my favorite apple tree, I experienced the marvel and value of other creatures as simple fact and found a place where my body belonged without effort, and my presence was not an intrusion or a mistake.

I spent hours watching metallic plum-backed beetles, pill millipedes, earwigs. And significant time learning and dispensing peer-to-peer neighbourhood natural history:

- a tiny round red beetle with black spots is a ladybug
- you can tell its age by counting its spots
- if one lands on you, blow it off and say, "Ladybug, ladybug fly away home"
- the additional words, "Your house is on fire, your children are gone," are optional
- a yellow spotted beetle or a black beetle with red spots is a manbug—there are not so many of these, and no recitation is required
- an earwig exists to crawl in your ear
- if successful, the earwig will eat through to your brain, causing instant death.

It is possible that I have some natural inclination toward the more "fanciful" aspects of the Bestiary.

My mostly mute encounters with wild places and creatures continued as a touchstone of authenticity for me in adolescence, as I tried on different ways of being in the world. As a university student I worked as a tree planter in north-central British Columbia. I wasn't very good at it, but I got to spend endless days outdoors with birds, Black Bear, Moose, and, on one memorable occasion, a Wolverine. I spent part of another summer at a remote camp in the Lower Tsitika Valley, cataloguing species as part of a Wilderness Committee campaign to save the valley from logging and to protect the adjacent territory of the Northern Resident Orca population. Activists, naturalists, and Indigenous stakeholders would visit on the weekends, but my most frequent visitor was a thieving Marten who managed to haul a one litre can of olive oil two metres up a tree.

As an adult, I am an enthusiastic but mediocre birder—I bring binoculars and a field guide most places, but I do not keep the serious birder's cumulative record of species, a life list. I am a sporadic volunteer at the Vancouver Avian Research Centre, a little nonprofit dedicated to protecting local bird habitat. Observing nature, but especially encountering animals in the wild, has been a consistent place of spiritual connection for me. When we meet to talk about my prayer-life, my spiritual director is tasked with asking me how often I have made time to be outdoors. Disciplined engagement with both the natural world and Christian spiritual practice may seem an unlikely combination in a modern North American context where creationists and climate-change deniers are sometimes the noisiest of my co-religionists, but my own spiritual practice, and that of my little wilderness church, is part of a growing movement that goes by various names: contemplative ecology, Wild Church movement, watershed discipleship. Christians and other seekers are finding in nature a place of spiritual encounter, and often as well, the conviction, courage, and companions to take action for climate justice, to care for and defend that place of connection.

While the Wild Church practice of worship outdoors and our concerns about climate change and species extinction are relatively new, there is a robust tradition of saints, mystics, spiritual leaders, and clergy whose practice of the natural sciences was core to their faith. Ten centuries ago, Benedictine abbess and mystic Saint Hildegard of Bingen authored botanical and medicinal texts. Two hundred years later, one of the earliest European proponents of the scientific method was Franciscan friar Roger Bacon, although he "borrowed" heavily from Muslim scholar Hasan Ibn al-Haytham. Beginning in the 1500s with William Turner, the ornithologist and "father of English botany," a long list of parson-naturalists, including William Darwin Fox, cousin and tutor of Charles Darwin, saw the pursuit of natural science as an extension of their religious vocation. For centuries, these amateur collectors and cataloguers of flora and fauna were at the forefront of British scientific knowledge and exploration. The 19th century founder of modern genetics, Augustinian friar Gregor Mendel, is remembered by many high school students as the monk who studied peas.

This book, this not-quite-Bestiary, springs from three sources: the long tradition of Christian naturalists, my own spiritual home in this Pacific

Coast or Cascadia bioregion, and a sense of urgency about the global loss of biodiversity.

In a chilling 2018 *New York Times Magazine* article, Brooke Jarvis noted a peculiarity in the way that we think and talk about the loss of animal life on our planet. In lamenting the enormous decrease in biodiversity caused by climate change and habitat destruction, we focus almost exclusively on the number of species extinctions, leaving aside the staggering number of individual creatures lost. Jarvis says, "What we're losing is not just the *diversity* part of biodiversity, but the *bio* part: life in sheer quantity." In recent decades, deforestation, agriculture, and the industrial production of animals for food have led to a devastating 60 percent drop in the global numbers of wild vertebrates, while the human population has exploded. The mass of humans is now an order of magnitude higher than the mass of all wild mammals combined.

Most writers addressing this loss of biomass focus on ecosystem impacts. My questions are more personal, more familial, perhaps more spiritual. We humans evolved alongside and lived in proximity to large numbers of wild creatures. European settlers' earliest accounts of the North American continent describe American Bison, Pacific Salmon, Passenger Pigeons, and other animal inhabitants with words like "armies," "teeming hordes," "a living mass." I want to know how we are impacted by the absence of these ground-trembling, sky-darkening, cache-raiding companions. In 1856, American poet and natural scientist Henry David Thoreau, grieving the loss of Lynx, Wolverine, Beaver, and Panther from his Massachusetts home, said, "I listen to a concert in which so many parts are wanting." My hunch is that modern North Americans' current spiritual alienation includes a kind of interspecies loneliness, a longing for the absent creatures who were once our companions and competitors. Indeed, in response to those who have begun to describe our era as the Sixth Great Extinction or the Anthropocene, the geological age dominated by human activity, sociobiologist and ant expert E.O. Wilson coined the haunting term Eremocine, "the age of loneliness."

The absence of our creature companions has impacted our collective imagination and memory. Young people cannot recall how much more wildlife there used to be. Researchers (initially oceanographers) have documented a phenomenon called shifting baseline, which causes us to underestimate the extent of harm caused to radically depleted ecosystems.

Let me explain with an example: what if, before she died, I had thought to ask my grandmother to tell me about the abundance of any living thing when she was a young woman?

Let's choose wildflowers. When she was 96, I took her for a drive on the family farm in Southern Alberta and picked her a bouquet of about a dozen different species. She took them from my hand and told me the names of every one.

If my grandmother had described for me the density and diversity of flowers she remembered when she arrived as a young farm wife, there would be many more than my dad remembered when he left the farm at age 18. And if I were to recall the number and diversity when I visited here in my late teens, my recollection would be fewer still. My daughters, turning 18 this year, would have an even smaller estimate.

The same applies to insects: my grandmother remembered hordes eating crops, I remember hundreds smashed against the windshield, but my daughters recall only very occasional encounters with large numbers— swarms of mosquitoes at summer camp, an outbreak of flying ants in our housing co-op courtyard.

The problem is that, for each successive generation, what we experience is the "new normal." We cannot imagine how things were in the generation before us, and we underestimate the extent to which things have changed. More important to my thinking for this volume, is the fact that we cannot be un-impacted—spiritually, socially, and emotionally—by this rapid decrease in the sheer number of our other-than-human companions.

I suspect that we are caught between behavior and physiology that evolved in interspecies company, on the one hand, and the changing baseline of our perceptions on the other. Put another way, I think that part of our human distress and collective alienation—perhaps most strongly affecting urban people—is that we are lonely for something that we cannot even remember having had.

Recalling times in my own past when I had been near large numbers of creatures—walking through a field of grasshoppers as a child, kayaking accidentally into a California Sea Lion migration route on a family vacation, stumbling off a school bus to watch salmon spawn at Goldstream Park—I began to plot out not so much an encyclopedic Bestiary, as an account of in-depth encounters with nearby creatures. I planned to take a year and visit as many large gatherings of animals as I could; in my notes I called it the Big Numbers Project.

I imagined one tidy visit, and thus one chapter, per month, but the creatures proved obdurate and quite resistant to my schemes. Planned chapters never happened, and unexpected population blooms lead to unanticipated chapters. Eventually I had to let go of my outline and allow gaggles of geese and murders of crows to set the pace.

Gaggle and *murder* are commonplace collective nouns that take us back to the history of Christian naturalists. Both terms first appeared in a collection credited to 15th century noblewoman-cum-nun, Dame Juliana Berners. Berners' *Boke of St. Albans* (the first book in English to be printed in more than two colours) is not quite a Bestiary but a treatise on falconry, hunting, and heraldry. An additional essay on fishing includes some of the earliest ideas about streamside habitat conservation and is the basis for Isaak Walton's 1653 *The Compleat Angler*. While Dame Juliana's biography is sketchy at best, the content of her "boke" seems to imply that taking religious vows did nothing to curb her outdoor pursuits, and in England and the United States, women's fishing clubs continue to be called "Berners" or "Julianas" in her honour.

In addition to murder and gaggle, Berners documented, or perhaps invented, these more fanciful collective terms as well: "unkindness of ravens," "exultation of larks," "siege of herons," "sword of mallards," "host of sparrows," and "charm of finches." Her collective terms for humans include some social commentary: a "melody of harpers," an "obeisance of servants," a "non-patience of wives," a "blush of boys," an "eloquence of lawyers," and a "superfluity of nuns." I must employ some of Dame Juliana's self-deprecation or perhaps an eye-roll as I look at the terms that might apply to me: a "prudence of vicars," a "discretion of priests," and a "worship of writers."

While linguists debate whether some of these terms were ever in common use, they make excellent chapter titles. And the collective name for these collective names, *terms of venery*, is, as one of my early readers remarked, a "deliciously old-fashioned" word for hunting. Venery also means carnal indulgence, which is also apt, given that when creatures gather in large numbers it is often with reproductive intent. Sockeye Salmon do it, Great Blue Herons do it, Western Toads do it, and my writing does not shy away from the creatures' frank excesses and the ways in which they are gloriously oblivious to human sexual mores and behaviours.

I hope, reader, that this journey through a year—wild, sacred, and profane—will inspire similar pilgrimages in your own watershed, and that it will find a small place in the great story of those who, like Hildegard and Juliana, loved the infinite by loving the very particular. Study of the natural world is an act of praise. When I see spawning Chum return to a restored creek, poke through River Otter spraints with a stick, or fasten a band on the toothpick leg of a Cedar Waxwing, no allegory or a moralizing object lesson is required; there is miracle enough right there. Creation, like scripture, is a word of God, and the Divine cannot be threatened by our knowing it better. Or, to quote a child I once knew—you can love the Lord *and* dinosaurs.

SOURCES AND RESOURCES

Aberdeen Bestiary

England, ~1200
An illuminated medieval compendium of beasts, their natural histories and moral lessons. The Aberdeen University has digitized the entirety of this manuscript in high resolution and made it available publicly. Beautiful, thorough, and easy to navigate.
abdn.ac.uk/bestiary

"The Biomass Distribution on Earth"

By Yinon M. Bar-On, Rob Phillips, and Ron Milo
Proceedings of the National Academy of Sciences of the United States of America, June 19, 2018, vol. 115 no. 25, 2018, pp. 6506-6511.
This technical scientific article on how life is distributed globally and the impact of humans on that distribution, is accessible to the adult layperson.

Boke of Seynt Albans

By Juliana Berners
Saint Albans Press, 1486
The text of Dame Juliana's treatises on hunting, hawking, heraldry, and fishing is available online through the University of Toronto's Lexicons of Early Modern English. New and used print and electronic versions are available from various other sources. The section on heraldry is the first example of colour printing in England.
leme.library.utoronto.ca/lexicons/22/details

The Compleat Angler

By Izaak Walton
Marriot, 1653
First published in 1653 and compiled from multiple sources, including Dame Juliana's St. Albans, this celebration of fishing includes technique, conservation, lifestyle, and humor. The book has been in almost continuous print for nearly 500 years and is available in forms from antique to e-book.

Curious Kids Nature Guide: Explore the Amazing Outdoors of the Pacific Northwest

By Fiona Cohen, illustrated by Marni Fylling
Sasquatch Books, 2017
A user-friendly guide for all ages to ecosystems of West Coast North America. Organized around familiar habitats—forest, beach, fresh water, parks—this book is full of fun facts.

"The Insect Apocalypse Is Here"

By Brooke Jarvis
New York Times Magazine, November 27, 2018
This intensive feature article uses the dramatic decrease in insect populations as a starting place to inquire deeply into human-caused degradation of the natural world. Jarvis relates with urgency windshield phenomena, shifting baseline syndrome, citizen scientists, and functional extinction in this, the Eremocene, or age of loneliness.

Letters to a Young Scientist

By Edward O. Wilson
Liveright (Norton), 2013
Written in the form of letters, this partial autobiography by eminent entomologist E.O. Wilson is a book about how passion and creativity are key elements of scientific endeavor and even human survival.

A Murmuration of Starlings: The Collective Nouns of Animals and Birds

Written and illustrated by Steve Palin
Merlin Unwin Books, 2013
Written in the form of an alphabet book and illustrated with watercolours, this collection of collective nouns pays particular attention to the development of language but focuses on birds and animals of Britain.

An Unkindness of Ravens: A Book of Collective Nouns

By Chloe Rhodes, illustrated by Aubrey Smith
O'Mara Books, 2014
Illustrated in stark black and white, this collection includes collective terms for wild and domestic animals, as well as humans. The focus is on history and language rather than natural history.

Vancouver Avian Research Centre

VARC is small organization dedicated to safeguarding local birds and their habitat through research, conservation, education. Research projects include a songbird banding station at Colony Farm Regional Park in Coquitlam, and several species-specific studies.
birdvancouver.com

What is Life?

By J.B.S. Haldane
Boni and Gaer, 1947
An out-of-print collection of political and scientific essays by the British geneticist and popularizer of science. Haldane was a vocal critic of how right-wing regimes used genetic theory as a pretext for apartheid systems and eugenics.

Wild Church Network

An informal association of mostly North American Wild Churches and their leaders, who meet for mutual support and share resources, theologies, and practices.
wildchurchnetwork.com

"Young people can't remember how much more wildlife there used to be"

by Adam Vaughn
New Scientist, December 11, 2019
A short, readable article describing the problem of shifting baseline syndrome.

A Haul Out of
Sea Lions

1

The watch—then headed by Flask—was startled by a cry so plaintively wild and unearthly—like half-articulated wailings of the ghosts of all Herod's murdered Innocents—that one and all, they started from their reveries, and for the space of some moments stood, or sat, or leaned all transfixed by listening, like the carved Roman slave, while that wild cry remained within hearing ... Below in his hammock, Ahab did not hear of this till grey dawn, when he came to the deck; it was then recounted to him by Flask, not unaccompanied with hinted dark meanings. He hollowly laughed, and thus explained the wonder. Those rocky islands the ship had passed were the resort of great numbers of seals, and some young seals that had lost their dams, or some dams that had lost their cubs, must have risen nigh the ship and kept company with her, crying and sobbing with their human sort of wail. But this only the more affected some of them, because most mariners cherish a very superstitious feeling about seals.

Herman Melville, 1851

We heard them before we saw them: high, honking barks carried in an unceasing chorus over a kilometre from the water, while occasional roars made a deeper, rumbling undernote. Arriving well after dark, we set out on foot from our hotel by my usual method of substituting confidence and luck for careful preparation; we followed the barking, triangulating across the idiosyncratic grid of a small town that curves along the shoreline.

My daughter's high school classmates called the trip to Powell River our "nerd vacation." When I asked if she wanted to come and witness the unexpected descent of 1,000 California Sea Lions on a Sunshine Coast mill-town, I was surprised that she said yes. She was in the final term of a heavy academic program, and a winter road trip with your mom to look at fat marine mammals is not the height of teen cool. Maybe I shouldn't have been too shocked: this was a kid raised on nature videos instead of cartoons, who was appalled to learn that her peers could not collectively name more than three shark species.

As soon as our zigzagging path through town took us out of range of street lights, Myriam clutched my arm nervously. She's a biology nerd but also a city kid. Raised in a housing co-op in Vancouver's Downtown Eastside, she has more street smarts than wilderness skills. As we stumbled through an unused parking lot and along a rutted gravel road, the sea lions' barking and roaring grew louder. The road sloped uphill above the shore. Intermittently, through gaps in the trees, we could see the water below and, against its reflective surface, a few lumpy silhouettes resting on floats and logs. At most we could see about 20 sea lions; I was there for the full 1,000 and pressed on.

On our right, the ground dropped away behind a chain-link fence. To our left, small roads branched off into the night. When a dark car passed, Myriam noted the driver's suspicious appearance. "Why is he wearing a cap at night, in winter? So you can't see his face." After about five minutes, another vehicle passed: "Did you see that? A pickup, with a tarp in the back. That is definitely for dumping bodies."

We continued up the hill, with occasional glimpses of sea lions below, but eventually the road was blocked by a high, wire-topped gate. When we turned around, I was confident that we could cut around the industrial area and take a side road down to the water. Myriam was equally confident that every turn-off harboured a serial killer with a tarp-lined pickup truck.

The bank at the edge of the road cut away steeply on the water side, so that we were nearly level with the tops of trees. A large, dark shape on a branch just above eye-level brought me skidding to a halt. I hoped it was a Great Horned Owl, but my daughter's more youthful eyes correctly identified a roosting Bald Eagle. Its white head against the pale sky was completely invisible to me.

The consolation of close proximity to some kind of wildlife and the reality that perhaps my crappy middle-aged vision might not make me the best leader for a nighttime cliff-side ramble in unfamiliar territory were sufficient excuse to postpone our search until morning. We made our way to Townsite, the part of the city with the longest settler presence. Powell River was named for Israel Powell, superintendent of Indian affairs for BC in the late 1800s. A notorious supporter of residential schools, he removed sacred artefacts from communities and was instrumental in the banning of the potlatch. The Tla'amin Nation have initiated a conversation and education campaign about changing the name of the town to better reflect the community's values. At a brewery housed in an old brick art deco post office we found our local hosts: Ron, a deacon and permaculturist, and Laura, a lawyer. Along with craft beer, fancy sodas, and snacks, we greedily consumed church gossip, a story about Freddy Mercury, and correct directions to the beach for morning.

We had set out from Vancouver in the mid-afternoon and spent about five hours in transit: drive, ferry, drive, ferry, drive. While the city of Vancouver and the town of Powell River are part of the same landmass and about 125 kilometres apart, the folded inlets and fjords of the coast make it impossible to drive from one to the other. I spent much of the trip afraid that the sea lions would slip into the water *en masse* and swim away before we arrived. My specific fear about whether the sea lions would have left Powell River is an echo of the persistent anxiety about all wild creatures that underlies this entire book—*will they still be there?*

Myriam and I had seen migrating sea lions before. For years, our extended family spent a week each November near Parksville on Vancouver Island, and in 2013 we had our first sea lion encounter. Hundreds of them were travelling north past our resort. We would watch from kayaks or the shore as they swam past Craig's Bay, pausing to bark as they rounded the point. They seemed to be making vocal contact with those ahead and behind on the migration, but it was clear as they raised their heads and shoulders up out of the water and looked directly at us, that they were communicating with us as well. Thrilled by that first encounter, we had gone looking for the sea lions every year since, but we had never seen them out of the water.

In the hotel I fell asleep to their ceaseless barking, imagining them on land but afraid they would be gone before I woke. In the morning, before I even opened my eyes, I was reassured by continued barking. Leaving Myriam asleep, I slipped out and drove to the beach.

The first sea lions I saw were resting in piles on a dock in the harbor, with others on floating logs, perhaps 80 or 100 in all. Their breath formed clouds above them as they snorted and coughed in the cold morning air. Then, as I moved closer, a rocky breakwater came into view and I saw the promised thousand covering its entire 250-metre length.

I couldn't stop grinning. There weren't many of us humans there in the early morning. The sea lions had been in Powell River for nearly three weeks, and for most residents the novelty had worn off. Whenever possible, I prefer to avoid social interaction with strangers and I find most eye contact to be aggressive (a social expectation which I manage by looking near people's faces), but on the shore I found myself deliberately catching people's eyes, so they could be happy about sea lions too.

How do you describe 1,000 sea lions? On the breakwater they were a beautiful patchwork of colours, ranging from a sleek almost-black when they emerged from the water, to tawny gold in the sun. Together they formed a landscape, noisy, rippling, climbing over one another: a wall of flesh. A mature male can weigh up to 450 kilograms or 1,000 pounds. Even a small sea lion is a lot of animal.

Their fur is short, their whiskers long; their eyes are shiny dark brown, and they have tiny, twisted ears on the side of their heads. At two and a half metres long, when they bend from their front flippers and "stand up," nearly half their length is off the ground. Their tapered shape seems concentrated at the front end. Thick rolls of flesh cover their necks and chests. They have long, jointed, flat front flippers and flexible spines that allow them to scratch their heads with their rear flippers and to execute streamlined turns under water. Sea lions are dish-faced, like Labrador Retrievers, making the cartoons and memes that describe sea lions as "dog-mermaids" seem remarkably accurate.

Not being the sportswoman's typical quarry, sea lions do not have a unique term of venery in Dame Juliana's "boke of huntyg." Neither do other early collections of "company terms" offer a solution. So, what collective noun fits sea lions best? Should it be a *pod*, like whales? They are, after all, marine mammals. Or a *pride* like lions? They travel in groups like lions, they roar, and they even have a mane (although not as well developed as those of South American and Steller Sea Lions). To me, with their long noses, light muzzles and variety of colours, California Sea Lions most closely resemble Black Bears. Several modern collections of collective nouns call a group of bears a *sloth* or a *sleuth*, both of which could fit. If we must play the game of land counterpart, then the common name for the South American Sea Lion is instructive. In both Portuguese and Spanish, it is called *sea wolf*—so perhaps a group of sea lions is a *pack*?

I dashed back to the hotel for a speedy breakfast and returned with Myriam. This time we smelled the sea lions before we saw them: an overpowering fug of wet dog and recently digested fish. A stinking, constantly barking mass of furry energy, they were an assault on the senses.

Their configuration had changed since early morning. The sun was on the beach and perhaps 50 individuals had moved off the breakwater and onto the sand. They were separated from the muddy parking lot and the now much larger crowd of observers by a pile of driftwood left by the high tide. Sunning themselves on the rocky breakwater and the industrial rafts, most lay close together, occasionally treading on another's tail or flipper. On the sand they were piled up deeper—cuddle puddles with heart-shaped noses all pointing the same direction. While they didn't seem to lie more than three deep, it looked uncomfortable for the ones on the bottom.

I was reminded of the dating aesthetic of certain gay friends who admire big men with plenty of hair. Like the pool-party photos my friend Chris posts from Provincetown's Bear Week, these bodies also rolled rather than rippled with solid, ample flesh. And indeed, a group of California Sea Lions this far north is a male-only gathering.

California Sea Lions practice a weak form of polygyny, the mating pattern where one male mates with more than one female. For a long time, researchers misunderstood California Sea Lion mating dynamics because they focused their attention on male aggression and assumed that sea lions like to do it on the beach. The reality is more complex.

Beginning in May, female California Sea Lions "haul out" of the water in large numbers to give birth on beaches on the Pacific coasts of the United States and Mexico. Each mother gives birth to a single pup, which she tends on land for about five days. Then the mothers alternate between periods of ocean foraging, which can last up to three days, and nursing their pups on shore for up to a day. In the crowded beach conditions, females aggressively defend their space and their pups from other females.

After the females have given birth and the pups are no longer newborns, the largest of the males establish and defend individual territories on land. Females move freely between these territories, avoiding males that are very aggressive or energetic. Between 21 and 30 days post-partum, females prepare to select a mate. They mill about in groups, mounting one another and the territorial males before they make a choice. Sea lion sex itself is notoriously private, seldom seen even by researchers studying it. Perhaps to avoid overheating or perhaps to avoid the prying eyes of both marine mammal scientists and large territorial males, sea lions most often mate after dark or in the water.

In species that practice strong polygyny, like baboons and wild horses, very few males reproduce with a large number of females, who exercise little choice in mates. Something more subtle happens with California Sea Lions. Some large males use aggressive displays to defend a mating territory on land for two to six weeks at a time, fasting while they do so. The larger the animal, the longer he can sustain a fast and avoid losing his territory. Marine scientists once thought that only these territorial males reproduce, but paternity testing of pups revealed some surprises. While it is true that the majority of males do not reproduce at all in a year, and that territorial individuals can father as many as three or four pups a year, it turns out that most pups are actually fathered by non-territorial males, probably during mating that takes place in the water. Neither are female California Sea Lions simply passive features in a large male's territory. A female sea lion exercises some reproductive choice; she may mate with the male who claimed the territory where she gave birth, she may move to another male's territory and mate with him, or she may mate with a non-territorial male in the water. In males, size is correlated with reproductive success, but so is simple attendance at the haul out. In other words, for males, in order to pass on your genes: be large if you can, but large or small, *be around*.

After mating season, adult male California Sea Lions travel to the northernmost end of their range for the winter, where they can bulk up without competing with females or their own offspring for food. Which brings us back to Powell River and the approximately 800 tons of male sea lion lolling in the sun.

Sea lions exhibit extreme sexual dimorphism, with males weighing up to three or four times what females weigh. Females are streamlined and almost cylindrical, while males have thicker necks, like lions (and even tom cats), and a protruding crest on their heads like gorillas, which develop as they reach sexual maturity at around four years of age. If these indicators were not sufficient to show that the Powell River sea lions were a group of males, the constant barking would do it. At any given time, two or three individuals in a group of ten seemed to be shouting, while the others slept on, oblivious. Adult female sea lions and pups do not bark but communicate with quieter contact calls. Some observers describe these calls as "bleating," but the recordings that I listened to, while definitely quieter than the males, sounded less like a flock of sheep and more like the screeching and moaning audio track for a cheap haunted house. Melville's eerie description rings true.

Speaking of haunted houses, my friend Cameron and I sometimes play a game we call, "What's That Skull?" It is not a very complicated game: one of us posts a photo of an animal skull online and the other person has to speedily and correctly identify it, with hints along the way.

One round of the game, transcribed, looks like this:

Cam:	Ta da! Go, what's that skull?
Me:	Mammal.
Cam:	Yes
Me:	Carnivorous. Not a rodent.
	Good-sized eye sockets ... hrmmmm
	Weasels, genus Mustela?
Cam:	Nope
Me:	Curious scapular, aquatic? stinky?
	can't really see the teeth ... kind of peg-like???
	Mongoose?
Cam:	Nope
Me:	Can you give me a continent?
Cam:	Native to Europe, Asia and Africa. Several species.
	Sometimes a pet.
Me:	Prickly?

Cam: Ding ding ding! It is a hedgehog,
         I don't know what species.

The pace and complexity of the game were significantly enhanced when Cameron got a job at the Beaty Biodiversity Museum. A brilliant project of academic public relations, popular science accessibility, and interdisciplinary research, the Beaty houses and displays for the public the University of British Columbia's collection of two million biological specimens. In addition to proximity to a whole lot of skulls, Cameron's job included enthusiastic interpretation in a little back room full of show and tell—Barn Owl wings, butterflies in glass frames, Sea Otter pelts, and a chance to look at dehydrated sea lion poop under a dissecting scope! Marine mammal researchers count and examine the squid beaks, and the lenses and ear bones (called otoliths) of fish to learn about their relative proportions in sea lion diets. The size and composition of these prey species' remains carry information about their age, habitat, and exposure to pollutants, and thus reveal secrets about the pooper's history, range, and ecological relationships.

A sea lion skull is about the size of a football. The incisors, canines and premolars are identifiable by size and position, but to my unpracticed eye seem barely differentiated at all. Sea lion teeth all look like worn-down pencils, pointed stakes of different lengths and sizes for stabbing and tearing prey, which is swallowed whole or torn into smaller chunks. Sea lion teeth start out white but turn black over a lifetime of laying down layers, like rings in a tree trunk. Isotope analysis of these rings can tell researchers about changing ocean conditions over an individual's lifetime.

California Sea Lions eat five to eight percent of their body weight in food each day. They feed on various fish, including anchovies, herring, salmon, rockfish, and hake as well as squid and octopus. In addition to accelerating rapidly and opening wide to bite their prey, hunting sea lions can also create a vacuum, actually *sucking hapless victims into their mouths!* Wild sea lions often feed in groups; California Sea Lions will follow hunting dolphins, taking advantage of their greater ability to detect prey, and Galapagos Sea Lions have been observed hunting cooperatively for tuna. On land they have no non-human predators, but in the water California Sea Lions are prey for Transient or Bigg's Orcas, and Great White Sharks. Returning to the question of a collective name, i.e. what do we call a group of sea lions? sex matters, as do age and location. *Colony* and *rookery* are modern terms that refer to breeding groups of male and female sea lions together, or to mothers and pups, usually on land. A *raft* is a group of sea lions in water. *Bachelor herd* is a term for groups of immature and non-breeding males in a species like horses that practice strong polygyny, but the Powell River sea lions were mature and immature individuals, including fathers. *Haul out* refers to both the behavior and location of sea lions coming to land, and, while not sex-specific, it is probably the most accurate term. Haul out is also an evocatively fleshy term, although, unlike my own struggles to exit a straight-sided pool or climb from the water onto a dock, sea lions appear to do less hauling and seem to pop up onto rafts and rocks like a cork.

Looking more carefully at the Powell River docks, I noticed that what I had mistaken for a pile of sandbags or sacks of cement on the industrial docks was actually a small number of Harbor Seals that had insinuated themselves among the much larger group of their much larger companions. Both seals and sea lions are species of *pinniped*, meaning feather-foot, and together with the Walrus they share a common terrestrial ancestor, a hunter that transitioned to a marine environment some 30 million years ago.

Seals and sea lions can be distinguished from one another by behavior and appearance. Sea lions and fur seals make up the family *Otariidae*: eared or walking seals. They have visible external ears and can swivel their hind flippers under them to move swiftly, walking or galloping on all fours, bellies well clear of the ground. The iconic performing seals are usually California Sea Lions, which can lift their flexible upper bodies high to "clap" or balance a ball. The sea lion's fur is shades of brown, while the Harbour Seals are mottled grey. Harbour Seals are members of the much more entertainingly named family *Phocidae*. Just ask your favorite elementary school student to say "seal" in French. When swimming, their low profile in the water, short snout, and rounded head distinguish them from dog-faced sea lions, who will lift head, neck, and shoulders out of the water to bark. Seals have tiny front flippers that do not swivel. On land, their bellies never clear the ground, and in the water they utilize a rear-wheel-drive to propel themselves forward by alternating their hind flippers. Sea lions clap their large fore-flippers to their sides and fly through the water in a thrust and glide motion.

The sea lions, with their size, smell, and volume, were unapologetically in our faces, while the seals were much more unassuming. They seemed to have a little more respect for one another's personal space. Sea lions craned their heads around to their own rear flippers and into one another's business, while the seals rested with heads and tails upraised, like contented dumplings.

Observers and scientists are divided about the ferocity of sea lions. The second century apocryphal text *The Acts of Paul and Theckla* recounts the adventures of the biblical St. Paul and a virgin martyr Theckla, who baptizes herself when thrown to ferocious sea mammals in the Roman arena. While seals are not, for the most part, aggressive, the sea lions in Powell River spent a lot of time facing off in one-to-one dominance displays. They lunged toward each other, open mouthed and roaring, they shook their heads back and forth, pushed one another with their chests, and then, with no resolution that was clear to me, they would stop and lie down together in cuddly boyfriend piles. Even in breeding season, California Sea Lions engage in more threats than attacks, and territorial defense takes the form of ritualized boundary displays, a bit like dogs running along opposite sides of a fence.

As the sun crept across the beach and more people arrived, the distance between humans and sea lions decreased. The sea lions were aware of us but mostly indifferent. If there was a sudden move, or someone came too close, they would all rise up, fast and threatening, bringing their heads to human eye-level. Most of the time they moved slowly, seeming to roll the plush flesh of their chests forward, and hitch their hind ends after—a wave of motion rippling down their massive bodies. When they moved quickly, though, emerging swiftly from the water, bellies off the ground, their status as quadrupeds was clear—sea lions can *run!*

At one point, a tugboat in the harbor came close to the breakwater's far side and 50 or 60 sea lions raced over the rocks and plunged into the harbor, each one's motion setting off a chain reaction among its neighbours. Even though they were 200 metres away, my heart pounded in awe at the massive wave of collective motion, bodies crashing into the surf.

In the late afternoon, after Myriam had caught up on homework in the hotel and I had toured our friends' new co-housing project on a blueberry farm, we came back to the beach with our human hosts for a final visit. There were fewer sea lions on the breakwater and more on the sand and in the bay. Alone or in small flotillas, they glided between the dock and the breakwater or swam in lazy loops parallel to the beach, some with enormous flippers raised like sails above the water to regulate their body temperature.

Despite my intention to experience large groups, I found the collective entity hard to take in, and I kept narrowing my focus to individuals, looking for unique features and identifying characteristics. There was Drooly Guy, with ropes of bloody saliva swinging from his whiskery chops; Tufty Head's pronounced sagittal crest made him look like a camel; Does Not Understand Pillows rested his huge head and neck uncomfortably on a log; Poser and The Model maneuvered themselves quite close to the crowd of photographers, as though angling for a spot in *National Geographic*; while Icky Eye, Toe Nail, and Snakey Neck all hung back a bit. Then there were individuals with scars and injuries: this one's right eye was swollen closed, while another had a foot-long gash in his side. Several seemed to have numbers or symbols etched or branded into their fur.

A little online investigation later revealed that the United States National Oceanic and Atmospheric Administration and State Departments of Fish and Wildlife have been hot-branding Harbor Seals and California and Steller Sea Lions for about two decades, having determined that it provides the best combination of lasting, non-invasive, and non-traumatic marking for research and monitoring populations. What I mistook for a discoloured toenail on one individual was another researchers' marker, a plastic flipper tag.

Sea lions and humans have interacted for centuries. Sea lion remains have been found in First Nations archeological sites on Vancouver Island dating back two thousand years, although they were not as significant in culture or diet as other marine mammals. All populations of eared sea lions (subfamily *Otariinae*) have experienced significant decline into the 20th century due to hunting by humans and depletion of prey species; most have a protected conservation status, but California Sea Lion populations are in better shape than those of their relatives.

The Japanese Sea Lion was hunted to extinction before 1975. The New Zealand and Australian Sea Lions are both considered species at risk, with declining populations of fewer than 12,000 each. The Galapagos Sea Lion has a similarly small population, but its numbers appear to be stable.

Steller Sea Lions, the other ottarid that shares the Salish Sea with California Sea Lions, have been reduced by an estimated 80 percent in their western population since the 1970s, although the numbers in the far north and off the coast of Asia seem stable. With protected conservation status, they have had something of a recovery but are still listed as a species of special concern in Canada, particularly as 70 percent of births in British Columbia occur in a single location: the Scott Islands, off the northwest tip of Vancouver Island, an ecological reserve that also provides nesting habitat for 40 percent of the province's seabirds!

California Sea Lions have experienced steady population growth over the past few decades, since gaining legal protection in both the United States and Canada. Indeed, their numbers have increased to such an extent that they can come into conflict with commercial fishers competing for the same depleted fish stocks, particularly salmon, Steelhead, and herring. The sea wolves of South America have experienced similar population trajectories: declining numbers due to hunting and loss of prey, partial recovery with protected status, and competition with humans for fish.

The hairy Powell River sunbathers, although their conservation status is that of "least concern" and their global numbers are over a quarter of a million, still face threats, some related to climate change. Sea lions can be injured or killed in fishing nets and lines. As a relatively long-lived (15–25 years) predator, high on the food chain, they can be harmed by the bioaccumulation of toxic chemicals and heavy metals. Sea lions are also vulnerable to changes in ocean temperatures. *El Niño*, the periodic warming of the Pacific Ocean, drives California Sea Lions' prey species north to cooler waters and can devastate rookeries when undernourished females cannot carry pregnancies to term, those that do give birth fail to produce sufficient milk, and underweight pups are forced to hunt in depleted waters before they are developmentally ready.

The sea lion haul out in Powell River was the largest in living memory—and the cause for much speculation and debate. As I focused on the sea lions and let fragments of nearby conversation drift over me, our much more extroverted host Ron, joined in, in both English and Spanish:

"I'm always worried when animals change their behavior."

"The refugee family from church came down and were just amazed."

"It means that there is a healthy enough marine ecosystem out there to support them. They wouldn't stick around if there wasn't food here for them to eat."

"It's climate change that's causing it; it's got to be."

"I feel like we're just so lucky to live here and experience this."

"They're crashing the herring and anchovy stocks. I think fishermen should be allowed to shoot them if they're feeding from nets."

After about 45 minutes of Myriam and I mutely admiring the barking sea lions, taking photographs, and occasionally pointing out the particularly cute or silly, our hosts (who admittedly had been down to the beach before) were stamping their feet, tucking hands under their arms and were, quite frankly, done. Myriam and I exchanged maniacal looks and I half-yelled, "I am never leaving!"

Laura, the lawyer, attempted a kindly intervention—"Would you like to walk back for a hot chocolate?"—to ensure that Myriam was not being held captive. I faintly registered her shaking her head no, and a flurry of thanks and goodbyes, but I mostly remember a further glorious hour and half as the setting sun reflected off the sea lions' fur, creating silhouettes that my photography, at least, failed to capture.

As the sun went down and the warm, fishy breath of that adamantly alive mass of creatures was again visible in clouds over their heads, I reflected on the day. My joy at the sea lions' unapologetic existence was like them; it was too big, too many, too much to allow for anything else. But I was aware of what a rare thing it was. One day is a tiny fraction of my year, my life; I wondered how I would be different if I experienced proximity to wild flocks and herds more often—would I be humbler, happier, or would familiarity breed contempt? And thinking of familiarity, of family, I was incredibly grateful to be there with my daughter, to witness her love of creatures, but I wondered too how she would remember that day. As her generation lives to experience more of the impacts of climate change, as ecosystems change, species and populations balloon and crash, what will our day with the sea lions, our nerd vacation, come to mean to her?

SOURCES AND RESOURCES

Beaty Biodiversity Museum

University of British Columbia

2212 Main Mall, Vancouver, BC, Canada

A natural history museum showcasing the university's collection of specimens, beautifully and engagingly curated and displayed. Great hands-on learning for kids and families.

beatymuseum.ubc.ca

Explore the Salish Sea: A Nature Guide for Kids

By Joseph K. Gaydos and Audrey DeLella Benedict

Sasquatch Books, 2018

This beautiful combination of photographs and text explores the unique marine ecosystems of the Salish Sea. It is aimed at middle schoolers but is appropriate for any age.

Marine Mammals of British Columbia

By John K.B. Ford

Royal British Columbia Museum Publications, 2014

This clear field guide, with an emphasis on identification, range, and natural history, includes photographs, colour illustrations, line drawings, and range maps.

Moby Dick

By Herman Melville

Harper, 1851

This literary leviathan chronicles a whaling captain's obsession, but it also includes 19th century settler grapplings with nature, technology, conquest, and the relationship between humans and the more-than-human world. Whether or not we read the book or view any of its subsequent interpretations, we live with the impacts and heritage of its ideas.

Ocean Wise Conservation Association

This not-for-profit organization promoting ocean health through education, research, and conservation is best known for having run the Vancouver Aquarium, but it also does marine mammal rescue, seafood education, shoreline cleanup, and plastics research.

ocean.org

"Weak Polygyny in Califorina Sea Lions and the Potential for Alternative Mating Tactics"

By Ramona Flatz et al.

Plos One, March 14, 2012

A scientific study on California Sea Lion paternity at two Gulf of California rookeries in a peer-reviewed open access online publication. The discussion section of this article is accessible to adult lay readers.

WILDLIFE CONGREGATIONS

A Murder of Crows

2

One for sorrow,
Two for mirth,
Three for a funeral
And four for birth

English Counting Rhyme, 18th century

In my denomination, before a clergy person is ordained, they are sent on
a retreat to prepare for this major life transition: a time of prayer, contemplation, and separation from their usual daily routine. In December 2012,
on my pre-ordination retreat, as I was headed back to the retreat house near
the Nicomel River in Surrey, I was caught up in a flock of roosting crows.
As I walked alone on a gravel road at dusk, hundreds of crows began to
gather on the power lines and rail fences all around me—cawing loudly.
With each step I took, the birds ahead of me would rise up and settle back
down, wrapping me in a cloud of beating wings that followed me down the
road. I felt a great excitement and wonder to be at the centre of so much
noise and restless action. It was a kind of stirring joy.

Crows tell me things. I know they are actually communicating with one another, but the cries of a mobbing flock call me to pay attention, to come out and see the one-eyed Barred Owl that has returned to the alley. The alarm calls and fixed directional stare of a lone crow in a Willow tree point me to a Mink skulking along the perimeter of Lost Lagoon in Stanley Park. On a grey and cloudy day, a pair of crows, each preening the other's head and neck feathers, remind me that spring is coming. In June, adult crows' agitated cries and repeated short dives toward the ground suggest I might want cross to the other side of the street. Mobbing is a behavior of crows and some other animals where potential prey species collectively harass a predator. Gulls and Fieldfares (a kind of European thrush) will vomit and defecate on a threatening individual with impressive accuracy and volume, while crows usually stick to loud alarm cries and diving attacks with feet or bill.

While polishing up this chapter one November morning, the persistent cawing of crows drew me out of my basement apartment into our communal courtyard. There were about 50 crows perched high in trees and on renovators' scaffolding. I couldn't see the object of their attention but I suspected the young Raccoon that had been sleeping on the rooftop and one of last year's nests.

One crow glided down from a big Magnolia to a rope that the construction workers used for hauling supplies. Gripping the rope, one foot above the other it settled its wings. For the briefest of moments it rested there, composed. Then slowly the weight of the bird and the rocking motion of its body caused the rope to move over the pulley above, sinking a little each time the bird called. Caw, drop, flap, caw, drop, flap the crow struggled to remain in place.

As I climbed the stairs to the top of the building, hoping to see who or what the crows were so upset about—it was the wrong time of year to be defending fledglings—the relentless cawing rose and fell in waves all around me. I found myself craning my neck upward, grinning, anticipating what the crows might show me. Close to the trunk of a Maple tree I spied a tiny Cooper's Hawk. The mob adjusted position, making passes closer and closer. The little hawk no bigger than the crows, trying to keep an eye on any potential attacker, stretched its neck so far up that it was looking behind itself.

I am not the only Vancouverite who has encounters with crows. My letter carrier neighbor brings a pouch of chicken livers on her rounds to feed them. She, the teenager Agnes in the apartment upstairs, and I all provide snacks for Alastor, the one-legged (well, one-footed, really) courtyard crow. When I give a special whistle, Alastor arrives to eat a row of cat kibble that I line up on the fence, but it's a one-way exchange. Alastor has twice given our upstairs neighbor the macabre tribute of a bird's leg, and then there's the little girl in Seattle who has an astonishing collection of beads, buttons, paper clips, and such delivered by the crows she feeds.

Crows are ubiquitous in the city and have become an icon of East Vancouver life: scrappy, inventive, shabby-chic, and perhaps more than a little cocky. Their silhouettes appear in street mosaics, murals, coffee shop signs, silkscreened T-shirts, and of course, tattoos. For a couple of years, Canuck, an East Van crow—habituated to humans because he was rescued as a fallen fledgling—had a huge social media following, captivating fans with his daytime adventures riding the Skytrain, visiting fast-food outlets, and on one notable occasion, flying off with the knife from a crime-scene. At night, Canuck would leave his human friend and fly east to roost with the other crows.

Towards sunset every night from fall until early spring, small flocks of crows begin to gather all over Vancouver—ten, twenty, thirty, increasing in number as they make their ragged way east. Fluttering like dark handkerchiefs against the blue sky, they form a cohesive but independent group, flying close together, then spreading apart, some faster than others. Like school children crossing a playing field, clusters form and disperse. Crows fly with a kind of rowing motion and rarely glide. On windy days, they play in the air currents, throwing their bodies against the wind, falling and catching themselves. Small groups merge and coalesce until an estimated 20,000 of them arrive at a common roost on Still Creek, where East Vancouver meets the City of Burnaby. In early February I made my first visit to the Still Creek Roost. Following directions from an article online, I arrived at a Costco parking lot about an hour before sunset—too early. There were 30 or 40 birds in bare trees beside the lot and as many again on the ground between the railway ties and beside the tracks. The birds on the ground were methodically picking up rocks and turning them over—looking for food, I assumed. When one flew off with an entire fast-food French-fry box grasped in its bill, my suspicion was confirmed. I was impressed by the size of the rocks that the crows cast aside—between the size of a golf ball and a chicken's egg. How could a bird of that size manage it?

Some bathed in puddles on a flat roof. Farther east, on the power lines and fences outside the city recycling station, were a few dozen more, attracted by the abundance of organics. One on a light post held half a chicken femur, picked clean.

The crows we see in Vancouver are Northwestern Crows, a species that lives along the Pacific coast in sparsely treed areas. Northwestern Crows typically feed in intertidal areas, wading out to catch small fish and marine invertebrates. But they are omnivorous and incredibly adaptive opportunivores, hunting a variety of small animals like amphibians, snakes, and songbirds, and scavenging fruit, grains, carrion, and garbage. They are nest predators who eat the eggs and young of both smaller and larger birds. The Chickadee nesting-box on the Cherry tree outside my window is a source of frustration every spring. Crows, who can hear the nestlings but not reach them, take it in turn to stand on the roof of the little house, bending over to insert their bills through the quarter-sized opening. Crows will steal food from humans, Bald Eagles, gulls, and other crows, and in times of abundance, like low tide, they cache food, hiding it for later. My friend Ron, our sea lion host, regularly sees a crow in Powell River that drops clams in front of passing cars then dives down to eat when the road is clear.

As with the sea lions, I found myself noticing the traits of individual crows: one was missing a primary feather, another sported puffy head feathers like the drummer from an '80s hair band, that one had an over-long upper bill. After about half an hour, there were still only about 100 birds. I could see that many in a park any day. As the numbers stayed static, I wondered, "Are they really coming? Maybe they've chosen a different place to roost tonight. Maybe this is it." I crossed the railway tracks, noticing the ties mounded with stones of some kind of reddish-black volcanic rock, full of holes and light enough for a crow to toss with ease.

As the light dimmed, more crows silently appeared: in the trees in the parking lot, on fences, perched on the handle of a shopping cart. I saw very few in the air. It was as though they materialized when my back was turned.

My perception, from years in Vancouver, was that the crows fly east to roost, so I scanned the skies to the west and climbed a concrete staircase to the overpass for a better view of the city. And they came in intermittent groups of 20 and 30. Then, as I looked behind me across the roof of Costco, across the lot where city-owned vehicles are parked, I could see a flickering cloud in the distance—moving and billowing, drifting left and right, separating, re-forming and slowly becoming more distinct. Finally, the glittering specks resolved into hundreds of birds flying west. And, unlike the silent specters already in the trees, they called to one another constantly.

I moved closer as wave after wave kept coming from the east. While there was not a ceaseless flow of birds overhead, for about an hour there was no point at which there were not crows in the air.

Standing beneath the waves, looking up at the silhouettes moving overhead, I was overwhelmed by their numbers. Suddenly I was swept with a feeling of certainty that, whatever happens to humans in this global ecological crisis, however the excesses of the few are suffered by the impoverished many, whatever number of species and habitats we take with us as our own numbers are decimated or extinguished, life—the energy, drive, and beauty embodied in these crows (whether Northwestern Crows as a species continue or not) cannot be stayed. And that in the face of that unstoppable life-force, humans, and this human in particular, are not very important. Perhaps that is not a very comforting sentiment, but I found myself profoundly reassured; it shifted my perspective towards evolutionary time. And in that shift, that reassurance, I heard the Divine voice.

Crows are members of the corvid family, a widespread group of passerines, or "perching birds," that in British Columbia includes Common Ravens, Steller's Jays, Magpies, and Nutcrackers. They have strong feet and bills and, pound per pound, are equipped with as much brain as great apes, whales, and dolphins. Corvids can solve multi-step problems; some make and use tools; and many keep track of complex social hierarchies. European Magpies even recognize themselves in mirrors. Studies with Scrub Jays have shown that if a jay knows it has been seen caching food, it will move the food to a new cache later, but only if that individual has stolen from others previously. In other words, it takes a thief to fool a thief.

Intelligent, social, and starkly coloured, corvids feature in various religious traditions around the world. Huginn and Muninn are ravens who carry information to the Norse god Odin. In Japanese Buddhism and folk practice, Crow Tengu are disruptive spirits depicted with crow heads on human torsos. In China, Korea, and Japan a three-legged crow is a deity or messenger who lives in the sun. The biblical prophet Elijah is fed by ravens. Here on the Pacific coast, in several Indigenous traditions, Raven is a powerful trickster. In the Qu'ran, a crow triggers the remorse of Cain, the first murderer, by showing him how to bury his brother.

In many bird identification guides, "crow-sized" is a common standard of measure. At 17 inches, or 43 cm, from the bill to the tip of its tail, a crow stands about as tall as a bowling pin. While most people are unlikely to mistake a crow for something else, there are a few birds in British Columbia that might be misidentified as crows by the unfamiliar or inattentive. Blackbirds and grackles are not corvids. They are smaller than crows, do not caw, have narrower bills, and are more slight and streamlined.

While they are called "blackbirds," their plumage is actually quite varied: females are often brown and males are shiny black with a bright flash of bright colour—shoulder patches on Redwings, bright yellow and orange on orioles, iridescent blues and greens on Brewer's Blackbirds and grackles. A more common mistake is to confuse crows with Common Ravens. Both are black corvids with a harsh call. Ravens are less social than crows and, except near food sources, are usually seen singly or in pairs; they are not intimidated by people but frequent urban areas less often than crows. So, if you see a large group of all-black birds, in a big city (but not at the dump), you can safely assume they are crows. Ravens are larger birds—about a crow and a half in length and more than two crows in weight—so if you see the two species together the difference is quite striking. For the more detail-oriented observer, Common Ravens have a thicker neck and bill and shaggier throat, and a proportionally longer and narrower tail. Crows make a harsh caw and occasionally a rattle sound. The Raven's call is more of a croak with a guttural, chuckling kind of undertone. They also have a much wider vocabulary than crows, including a slow cluck that sounds like dripping water.

As the parent of identical twins, I am well aware that these kinds of differentiations are only really helpful to the uninitiated when the two look-alikes are present together. Last year, the youths and camp elder at our church's leadership program used this handy mnemonic to distinguish between crows and ravens in flight: a crow's tail is short and rounded at the end, like the letter "C" in crow. The raven's tail is longer and described in field guides as wedge-shaped, resembling a "V," as in raven. With these reminders and practice, the differences quickly become obvious.

A more subtle distinction is the differences between our coastal crows and the slightly larger American Crow, which occupies the rest of the continent. Although it is smaller, the Northwestern Crow has a harsher, deeper, more nasal voice than American Crow. Sometimes when I travel, I am startled to notice how different the American Crow sounds to my not-very-discerning ears. The Cornell Lab of Ornithology describes the

Northwestern Crow's call as a "craah" versus the American Crow's "caw." To me, the vowel in our local crows' call sounds more like the short-"A" sound in "cat," where the American Crow has a brighter sound, with a vowel more like "hawk" or "box."

Crows have been congregating near Still Creek since the 1970s. In winter, the roost is at its peak size, with adults and hatch-year birds together. In 2019 a frequently quoted news article estimated there were 20,000 individuals; my sources say about 15,000, although other observers claim fewer still. Roosting in the thousands is a recent phenomenon that seems to be a response to a combination of factors: habitat loss, access to urban food sources, and the defenses against predators provided by city lights and critical mass. Crows are one of the species that urban ornithologists call "exploiters"; their ability to adapt to and thrive in conditions created by humans has increased their reproductive success.

The Costco parking lot is one of several "pre-roost" areas where the crows spend their final half-hour before bed. A block from the overpass where I first watched the crows arrive is a pedestrian and bicycle path that follows Still Creek itself. Along the street, crows line the power lines like beads on a string, and the noise is constant. I followed the pathway down into a tiny greenway where the branches of bare deciduous trees reached for the sky and every tree was filled with crows, thousands of them, more every minute, calling back and forth, settling, and changing position.

My powerful sense that crows, and indeed life itself, will carry on however humans trash this planet, puts me in mind of certain biblical passages. Scattered throughout the oracles of prophets and the lyrics of psalmists are warnings of the woe and desolation that await those whose faithfulness is lacking. The fate of those who demonstrate their lack of faith by failing to care for vulnerable members of society, neglecting the minutiae of prescribed worship practice, or whoring after alien gods, is occupation: ravens, jackals, thorns, and owls will occupy their cities.

The creatures that the prophets name, are the "exploiters." They are scavengers and co-existers. Liminal like crows, Coyotes, and Himalayan

Blackberry, they are the ones who will expand to fill the vacant niche when we humans have self-destructed. Biblically, the night creatures' and carrion eaters' occupation of the city is intended to demonstrate how the wicked will be annihilated, but it gives me a subversive kind of hope. It is an inadvertent testament to the resilience of creation; whatever humans do, these scripture passages proclaim, the more-than-human world will inevitably reassert itself—if there are corpses in the street, for a while at least, the crows will do well.

And for that reason, not everyone is delighted by their crow encounters. I can only entice my partner to the Still Creek Roost if she gets to stay in the car. The scene in the Costco parking lot brings to mind Alfred Hitchcock's film *The Birds*. Occasionally crows will gather around their dead in order to identify threats and predators, and on rare occasions they will mob an interloper to death—behaviours that have led to stories of crow funerals, trials, and even executions. These stories, along with crows' penchant for carrion, including that from human battlefields, robbing nests, damaging crops, and tearing up suburban lawns, have given the birds a bad rap.

Around one percent of the United States' population experiences ornithophobia, or fear of birds, and I'd guess about the same for Canadians—or even more, as we're more likely to have to contend with Canada Geese. For many people, the phobia stems from a frightening experience with birds in childhood: a panicked bird trapped in the house, a flock of seagulls going after your French fries, a mishap in a hen-house, or, as happened to my young neighbor several years ago, being identified as a threat to offspring and attacked by a mob of crows. One spring morning, I found Joey, age seven, in the centre of our co-op's courtyard, surrounded by crows and screaming bloody murder.

Murder, as a collective name for crows, appears by the 1400s in lists of these terms. Dame Juliana's *Boke of Seynt Albans* does not include crows, but she called a group of ravens "an unkindness" and, unlike the more fanciful "exultation of larks" or "charm of goldfinches," murder satisfies the lexicographers because it is a word in common usage. As Joey turned in a circle, about 10 or 15 crows swooped down from trees and railings on all sides, clipping his ear or batting his head with their wings whenever he turned away.

The perception of many people is that attacks like this are either random—crows just sometimes attack people—or continuous—crows are always on the look-out for an opportunity—neither is true. Two geography instructors at Langara College have developed a Geographic Information System to track crow attacks: an interactive, user-generated map that documents the location and severity of crow-human (and sometimes crow-dog) interactions in the metro Vancouver area. And the patterns are very clear.

In the spring and summer months, numbers at the Still Creek crow roost drop as crows attend to the business of making more crows. In late February and early March, I begin to notice crows sitting together in twos on power lines and tree branches, gently nibbling at the feathers on each other's head and neck, a behavior called *allopreening*, which reinforces the bond between a mating pair. Crows form long-term pair bonds, although they are not entirely strict practitioners of monogamy.

Some field guides indicate that male crows are slightly larger or heavier than females. This is not a difference that I can detect, but my upstairs neighbor Agnes has recently informed me that the one-legged Alastor is a female and her mate is huge by comparison.

Apparently a pair of crows will visit several possible nesting sites before selecting one, often near a previous year's nest or in the territory claimed by that pair or their extended family. Over several years, I have had the good fortune to observe crows nesting in and around our courtyard in Vancouver's Downtown Eastside. Popular nest sites include two Cherry trees, the one with the chickadee box outside my door and another over the children's playground, a Maple tree, a Magnolia tree, and the Little Leaf Lindens that line Powell Street. On the side of a neighbouring building, a nest appears each year on a cluster of those periscope things for electrical wires, which I have since learned are called *weatherheads*.

My best friend, who is (not by coincidence) my children's father, lives in our co-op across the courtyard in a brick building more than 100 years old. Bolted onto the outside of the building below the windows are pretend balconies—metal structures that suggest a balcony but are only big enough to support a flower pot. While some neighbours hang compact disks, pie pans, metallic streamers, and other reflective material from these railings, for the past several years Bruce's not-balcony and another on the east side of the building have defiantly played host to crows' nests.

By the end of March, it seems like every second crow is carrying a stick. Crows begin their nests by constructing a rough platform of sticks, some as long as sixty centimetres. Crows in Japan have been photographed stealing wire clothes hangers and using them to build the outer structure of their nests. On my side of the courtyard, the nests in trees are mixing-bowl-sized, much larger than the soup bowl efficiency apartments sized to fit the not-balconies. As the nest progresses, the materials inside become narrower and more flexible: willow branches, roots, vines, grasses, as well as plastic zip-ties and fishing line.

During this time the pair, and sometimes a nest helper, an offspring from a previous year who is not yet breeding, will defend the territory from predators—raptors, Raccoons, Skunks. Often in the early morning, the harsh defense cries of crows echo off the buildings. In some places, like our courtyard, pairs will tolerate the proximity of neighbours for the advantage of mutual defense. We usually have at least two nests and sometimes as many as five. Together, those crows drive off both predators and other crows.

I have observed that, during nest-building, incubation, and fledging, crows are cautious about humans but not aggressive. I have stood a scant metre and a half away from a nest, photographing hatchlings for 30 minutes at a time and been observed sternly but not threatened or attacked.

Crows lay between three and six beautiful pointed eggs, of a size and shape that would fit perfectly into a teaspoon. They are a blue-green with dark, brownish grey splotches. After two and a half weeks, the chicks hatch: bald, pink, blind, and helpless. Crows, like other songbirds, invest a short period of very intensive care and energy into their offspring, who develop rapidly and, after only two more weeks, are capable of flight.

A crow's first flight is really more controlled falling. Blue-eyed, wide-mouthed, with light shining through their wings, they make an initial flight to the ground or perhaps to a lower branch. They can't fly back to the nest and are pretty much devoid of defensive skills. This is when all hell breaks loose. Unless a nest fails, the pair will not mate again until next year. Parents have invested all their reproductive efforts in these helpless feathered baseballs, on or near the ground.

Although they occasionally attack humans at other times of the year, it is in May and June, when their vulnerable young are learning to fly, that crows are the most aggressive. And that is what happened to Joey: he crossed the courtyard to visit a friend when there were fledglings on the ground. Parents and perhaps a nest helper identified him as a threat and attacked. His cries and theirs alerted other nesting pairs or cooperative breeders in the courtyard, who joined in with the mobbing behavior.

I dashed out, yelling at the crows, and hustled Joey inside.

Now, the tricky thing is that crows are very smart. Recent studies in Seattle have shown that crows can recognize and remember human faces; a human identified as a threat will be repeatedly scolded and attacked, not just for that nesting season but in subsequent (nine and counting) years. Crows who witness this protective behavior will join in, memorize a face, and treat that human as a threat in future encounters, amplifying the protective response.

You can see where those who are already nervous about crows or inclined towards nightmares inspired by Hitchcock or Poe might feel threatened. But it is worth noting that crows do not, as some people suppose, put out an all-points bulletin or pass around the descriptions of those they identify as dangerous. Crows need to witness the threat response before they take it up. They need to have the threatening individual pointed out to them.

Although they leave the nest a month after hatching, crows have a relatively long childhood—parents feed them for another couple of months, and they are not sexually mature until about 20 months. Juvenile crows will engage in play activities, including manipulating objects, caching non-food items, aerial acrobatics, and sliding on inclined surfaces. Play is incredibly rare in birds and is likely related to the juveniles' developing intelligence.

I love many things about crows: their shiny feathers, the wealth of detail and subtlety in the colour black, and their seeming sameness but the remarkable difference between individuals. They are confident, inquisitive, hilarious; I once saw a crow on a playground hide a stolen Oreo under a pile of leaves. I love their interactions with one another, with humans, with other species. They are extremely relatable and at the same time quite alien. Perhaps what I love most of all is that they are so ordinary—I see crows every day, and the crow roost, this miracle of the assembling thousands, is completely accessible. They are not shy or "exotic"; you do not require special equipment to see them or have to travel any distance; no years of meditation techniques, no religious functionary's mediation are needed. Ride a bus to a box store parking lot for straight-up access to the Divine in the heart of the city.

SOURCES AND RESOURCES

British Columbia Rare Bird Alert

A blog-style website that provides up-to-date information on rare and noteworthy bird sightings in the province of British Columbia. Moderated by Melissa Hafting (@bcbirdergirl)
bcbirdalert.blogspot.com

Cornell Lab of Ornithology

This online guide to more than 600 North American species of bird includes photographs, audio recordings, range maps, and life histories as well as courses for all ages and skill levels, bird cams, citizen science projects and a free bird identification app.
allaboutbirds.org

Corvids Literature Database

This ambitious project aims to record and make searchable 500 years of published scientific and popular literature on crows, ravens, jays, and magpies, extant and extinct. Developed and maintained by Gabi Droege, it currently includes publications from 164 countries in 36 languages.
corvids.de

Crow Boy

By Taro Yashima
Viking, 1956, Puffin, 1983
An illustrated children's story about a mountain boy who is excluded by his peers but learns the language of crows. Written under a pseudonym by Japanese artist Atsushi Iwamatsu, who lived in the USA during World War II.

Crow Smarts: Inside the Brain of the World's Brightest Bird

By Pamela S. Turner
Houghton Mifflin Harcourt, 2016
This juvenile non-fiction book, illustrated with colour photographs, will engage readers of all ages with clear explanations of the latest research on corvid intelligence.

Crow Winter

By Karen McBride
Harper Collins, 2019
Algonquin Anishinaabe writer Karen McBride's novel about family, grief, resource extraction, and a shape-shifting crow.

"Crows of Vancouver: The Middle Way Between Biophobia and Biophilia"

By Christine Thuring
The Nature of Cities, April 16, 2019
An engaging article by an ecologist and activist on the joys and challenges of living with greater Vancouver's Still Creek crows, published in an international online magazine on green cities.

CrowTrax Crow Attack Tracker

A user-generated mapping project that tracks the location, frequency, and severity of crow attacks in Vancouver and Victoria, created by Jim O'Leary and Rick Davidson of Langara College.
giscourses.net/crowtrax/crowtrax.html

"Murder Mystery: The Reason Why 6,000 Crows Flock to Burnaby Every Night"

By Susan Lazaruk
The Province, October 24, 2013
An accessible Halloween-inspired article on the Still Creek Roost, based on interviews with local ornithologists.

Raven Brings the Light

By Roy Henry Vickers and Robert Budd, illustrated by Roy Henry Vickers
Harbour Publishing Company, 2013
The picture-book version of a Haida origin story that is thousands of years old, is illustrated by celebrated artist Roy Henry Vickers.

"Where Do the Crows Go?"

By Paul Silveria

Bandcamp, 2020

On the album *Two Dollar Bill* old time banjo player, songwriter, and square dance caller Paul Silveria (aka Professor Banjo) compares the nightly flight the East Van crows and the annual migration of Vaux's Swifts of Portland, Oregon, to a travelling musician leaving and returning to his love. The song expresses wonder and delight at the movement of urban wildlife.

WILDLIFE CONGREGATIONS

A Siege of Herons

3

I visited a large colony of herons on Horse Hummock on April 27, 1888. Several hundred pairs were nesting there at the time. Most of them were little blue and snow herons, with some white egrets, Louisiana herons, and black-crowned night herons. When quite close to the breeding-grounds I climbed a tall gum tree, and being partially screened by the thick foliage was able, unobserved by the birds, to survey the scene at leisure ... Three years later I again visited the heronry at Horse Hummock, found the old gum, and climbed among its branches. But the scene had changed. Not a heron was visible. I discharged my revolver, but the answering echoes and the tapping of a woodpecker were the only response. The call had come from Northern cities for greater quantities of heron plumes for millinery. The plume-hunter had discovered the colony, and a few shattered nests were all that was left to tell of the once populous colony. The few surviving tenants, if there were any, had fled in terror to the recesses of wilder swamps. Wearily I descended from the trees to find among the leaves and mould the crumbling bones of slaughtered birds.

T. Gilbert Pearson, 1897

In mid-March, a friend posted on Facebook, "the herons have arrived." A few days later, I charged my camera battery and hopped on a bus headed for Vancouver's oldest, largest, and best-known park. For more than a century, a massive group of Great Blue Herons have nested on this peninsula in the Burrard Inlet. Their tenure overlaps that of the longstanding Squamish villages and immigrant Hawaiian, Portuguese-Squamish settlements and Chinese batchelor homes that were displaced to make Stanley Park, intended as a nature retreat for Vancouver's white working class. The rookery has been at its current spot near English Bay for nearly 20 years. The herons return every spring, but the precise timing of their arrival and subsequent mating varies from year to year, depending on the available food.

Great Blue Herons, solitary hunters, slow-motion stalking on the margins of lakes, streams, ditches, and ocean shores are a familiar sight across North America, even to those who have little interest in birds. Their slate-grey plumage, tufted heads and S-shaped necks are featured on the logos of beer companies, casinos, golf courses, retirement communities, and resorts, often in an attempt to sell some version of waterside tranquility. At nearly one metre tall, with continental numbers in the high tens of thousands, Great Blue Herons are hard to miss.

I've seen herons in Minnesota, Ontario, Florida, California, and Mexico. But the park herons are members of a local subspecies. *Ardea herodias fannini,* the Pacific Great Blue Heron, is a smaller, darker bird that lays fewer eggs than its relatives on the rest of the continent. Their range extends from Washington State to Alaska, but more than two-thirds of the Pacific Great Blue Heron population are concentrated around the Salish Sea, with the greatest density in the Fraser River delta. Although this area is densely populated by humans, there is abundant food in the river delta for herons. Unlike other Great Blue Heron sub-species, who are considered partial migrants, traveling south of their nesting range (but not far) in winter, the Pacific subspecies stays put year-round. Due to nesting failure, Bald Eagle predation, habitat loss, and human-caused disturbances, they are a blue-listed, or vulnerable, species with fewer than 5,000 individuals in Canada.

Herons are usually solitary birds, but outside of breeding season, in locations where food is plentiful, they will feed in proximity to one another. Dame Julian's 1486 "boke" says the proper term for a company of "herronys," as well as for their shyer, stockier relatives, the bitterns, is a "sege." In the subsequent centuries, this collective noun has been interpreted both as sedge (a genus of wet-growing, triangular stemmed grasses) and siege for both birds. I am swayed by the argument that *sedge* is a better fit for the more specific reedy habitat of the bittern, and *siege* suits the heron's patient hunting technique. But I admit that I am mostly swayed by my delight in the word. If I am not besieged by herons, I am certainly besotted—by their awkward grace, their focused stab-and-grab hunting technique, and some of their fascinatingly disgusting habits (more on these to follow).

We in Vancouver are incredibly lucky. Great Blue Herons are typically shy and will abandon a nesting colony if humans are too close or too loud. The park herons, in contrast, are supremely unperturbed by the almost constant stream of automobile, foot, and bicycle traffic flowing beneath their nests. A friend of mine regularly and gleefully recounts seeing a dinner-platter-sized heron shit landing in an open convertible that had stopped—in front of one of many "no stopping" signs—below a nest.

Although noisy and messy, the birds are mostly beloved by neighbours, who feel privileged to have this kind of access to wilderness in the city. Since 2015, the park has mounted a camera nearby so that footage from 40 of the nests can be viewed on a live stream. More than 100,000 viewers have visited the herons this way.

After leaving the bus on Georgia Street and cutting through the park, I was a bit disoriented. I had visited the heronry before but always approached from the water side. I walked, head up, scanning the bare trees ahead of me for nests. It turns out they were not too hard to find: perhaps 100 large, untidy nests in fewer than 20 big, bare deciduous trees, starting at about three stories high.

A note about numbers: in planning this book I had to decide what actually counts as a large number. Somewhat arbitrarily, I decided that 1,000 would be my cut-off point. I would aim for gatherings of 1,000 or more creatures, even if I did not lay eyes on each individual. The heronry falls well below that number. Statistics from the past 10 years indicate that active nests in the park have numbered in the mid-80s, and successful fledglings fewer than 120. If we add that up—two adult herons per active nest and 115 fledglings, even if we include 100 fledglings who didn't survive and perhaps a dozen unpaired adults—the total wouldn't be much more than 400. I could easily find a larger gathering of pigeons, gulls, or Canada Geese without too much effort. But the combination of the herons' preposterously large selves and the exceptional nature of this nesting site in the city led me to break my own rule.

As I got closer, I could see that massive skirts of some flexible metal had been fastened around the base of each tree, about a metre from the ground. I assumed these were to frustrate the bands of park Raccoons who have switched from nocturnal to daytime foraging, the better to bully and harass tourists out of their lunches, and who in 2009 attacked heron eggs and chicks in approximately 40 nests.

In the trees overhead, the nests were silhouetted against the sky, some a metre in diameter and half a metre deep, others just a ragged handful of sticks. Next to 20 or 25 of the nests, a long, grey oval was stationed, motionless and silent as a gravestone. The only sound was an occasional splatter of white on the ground or a low, grunting call. Perhaps every 10 minutes a heron would arrive, unfolding its neck, drawing in its wings, maneuvering its long legs from horizontal to grasp a branch. Then negotiating with its momentum, it would bounce on the branch, slowly flapping its wings to a standstill. This was both impressive and less exciting than I had anticipated. In previous years' visits I had seen more herons, and it felt like more was going on.

Herons are seasonally monogamous; they choose a new mate each season. A few nest as isolated pairs, but most breed in colonies called rookeries or, more specifically, heronries. A mating colony has certain advantages: some mutual defense against predators and a number of prospective mates all in one place. In the early spring, males leave their intertidal feeding areas, gather, and stake out nesting sites, most in trees. Females arrive one to two weeks later, and after that, courtship begins. It occurred to me that the relatively staid scene in the park might have meant that the males had established their territories but the females had not yet arrived.

Just as I was wondering at the quiet, a dramatic increase in volume and tempo from the treetops caused me to look up. Suddenly all the herons lifted off together, emitting high, insistent squawks, and took to the air, heading west. It was as though someone had lifted a blue-grey umbrella up above the height of the canopy. There were many more birds than I had imagined, 40 at least, all erupting from the trees and moving together toward English Bay.

A Bald Eagle cruised five to 10 metres above the tops of the trees, turning its head to look at the nests below. It flew close enough so I could see the yellow of its talons, but it did not make any aggressive moves towards the nests. The eagle had barely passed when herons began circling back to the rookery, re-establishing their places, making rattling calls as they landed.

*　*　*

My next visit, a few weeks later, was quite different. It was a weekend, and sounds of activity came from every direction—automobile traffic, picnickers, bicycle bells. It took me a minute to distinguish the herons' sounds from the background noise: squawks could be mistaken for the high-pitched yipping of boutique dogs on leashes, grunts like those of middle-aged tennis players on the courts below, and once every few minutes, a sound like a child's plastic shovel scraped over concrete. After I heard them, I began to see them as well. The trees were full of activity:

herons circling the trees, shaking their long necks, maneuvering with large sticks, touching down and taking off, and clattering their bills together. Shit and sticks fell around me. Clearly, the females had arrived and courtship was in full and raucous swing.

Male herons are slightly larger than females, but most observers distinguish between them by behavior. As spring approaches, herons undergo changes in their appearance. Field guides say the lore, skin between their eyes and bills, changes from blue to green, and their legs and bills go from yellow to more red tones with orangey pink, but the most noticeable trait of breeding herons, and the only one that I can easily identify, is the long, thin plumes on their heads, chests and backs.

In the late 1800s and early 1900s, breeding herons were hunted for these plumes, for use in the millinery trade. In 1902, the London Commercial Sales Room auctioned 1,608 30-ounce packages of herons' plumes, the equivalent of 192,960 living birds. Florence Merriam Bailey, an early conservationist and the author of the first ornithological field guide, *Birds Through an Opera Glass,* campaigned against the killing of birds for hats by promoting bird-watching as a suitable activity for young women.

In the trees above, herons were vigorously "shaking their plumes," so to speak. During the winter months, Great Blue Herons are solitary hunters and will warn others off their territory with defensive displays. For such habitually aggressive individuals to negotiate the close contact required to mate and care for chicks, they have developed complex rites for approach and bonding: the seemingly chaotic activity in the trees above was in fact a choreographed sequence of interactions being repeated asynchronously by different individuals and pairs.

Past seasons' nests adorn the trees year-round. While the males arrive first and stake out territory for the season, it is not clear to me whether they actually choose the nest or just a general area, with the female involved in nest site selection. Once a territory is secured and the females have arrived, the males begin a series of mostly visual maneuvers to showcase their attractiveness: neck-stretching, wing-shaking, bill-pointing and snapping, and flying in slow circles around the colony, neck extended. Impressed females will approach a male and be rebuffed, sometimes for a period of days. When the herons have narrowed their choices, courtship continues between two individuals, with displays of ritualized aggression and increasing proximity: both birds fluff their plumes, extend their necks, and clatter their bills together. The male will then collect sticks and offer them to the female. Accepting a stick seems to affirm a female's choice of mate. Above me a dozen herons were flying in with sticks collected from nearby trees, while others enterprisingly raided unoccupied, and presumably unclaimed, nests. Females accept the sticks and either start a new nest or weave them into a nest from previous years, which grow larger over time.

The Great Blue Heron combines a wingspan of nearly two metres with the weight of a Chihuahua. With as many as 20 in a tree, their nests are so crowded together, that a bird arriving with a metre-long branch inevitably smacks its mate, and a neighbour, or a neighbour's nest, with wingtips, stick, or both. With their snakey necks and outsized bills, this slow-motion aerial ballet looks like a scene from *Jurassic Park* or *King Kong*.

Right at the base of the trees, with a very modest lens on my camera, I had no chance at the beautiful nest shots that I saw others posting online. Neck craned back, camera in front of my face, I side-stepped into a pair of dog walkers and stumbled off the curb. There was not a lot of traffic that day, but I often think there are worse ways to go than being struck by a car while contemplating birds. Watching wildlife, particularly photographing or observing birds, is the only time when I have no internal dialogue, when I am fully and completely present to what I am doing and nothing else.

* * *

I visited the heronry again about a month later, in the middle of the day. There was a distinct fishy smell in the air, and the ground was splattered white with droppings. The trees had leafed-in a bit and the Big Leaf Maple branches had yellow-green fans at their tips, like flimsy pompoms. Many nests were clearly occupied, with one or two birds sitting in them, but the scene was subdued and less urgent; fewer birds calling or flying to and from nests.

Despite the diminished activity, there was plenty going on. One pair engaged in some courtship behavior, clattering bills together and preening their neck feathers. Another heron circled the rookery and, instead of making for the branches above, landed in the fenced-off area beneath the trees and began picking at a pile of sticks. After some wrestling and pecking, he removed a stick, flew up and presented it to his mate, who incorporated it into their nest. Realizing that the pile was a fallen nest, I moved in, hoping for a closer look at the inside. Herons line their nests with moss, leaves, or reeds to form a soft cup in the centre, but either the nest had been damaged in the fall or it had landed upside down. All I could see was an undifferentiated, footstool-sized ball of sticks.

Looking back at the treetops, I witnessed a painful 10-minute ordeal in which a male attempted over and over again to present a stick to a female on the nest. Hopping awkwardly to branches above and below her, each time he extended his offering, his neck, the stick, his bill, and hers were repeatedly blocked or entangled in the branches.

Another pair was mating on the edge of their nest. Birds do not have external sex organs. Both male and female birds have a cloaca, an internal chamber with tracts that lead to both reproductive and excretory organs. During mating season, the opening of the cloaca swells and extends outside the body. Heron sex is frequent, precarious, and swift. The male initiates, placing one foot on the back of the female. An unreceptive female simply does not respond; she carries on with other activities like nest-building or jabs at her mate with her bill. A receptive female crouches and the male hops on her back, flapping his wings for balance. The female shifts her tail feathers (or retricies) to the side, and the male may grasp her neck with his bill for balance; then he wags his tail back and forth so their cloaca brush by each other. Twenty seconds and done. If sperm is transferred from the male to the female, it is stored in the oviduct and will be used to fertilize eggs when they are mature. With such an unreliable method of transfer, herons mate repeatedly during the time that they are paired, usually in the morning and the evening. So a daytime mating is relatively rare.

With so much happening around me, I didn't know where to focus my attention. It felt like I was turning in a circle, just catching the action out of the corner of my eye and missing so much of what is going on.

The alarm calls of crows drew my attention, and I saw a pair of them harassing a lone heron, cawing loudly and sweeping in to dive at its head and shoulders, the larger bird jabbing back with its sword of a bill. I don't know how the altercation started, but it looked to me like the crows were the aggressors. Like Raccoons and Bald Eagles, Northwestern Crows will raid Great Blue Herons' nests for eggs and hatchlings.

Unlike crows, herons do not cooperate socially to defend their offspring, and as the nesting season progresses, their defensive response to attacks from predators does, too. Early in the season, as I observed in March, the whole colony launches into the air with alarm calls when an eagle threatens. Once the chicks have hatched, only the herons in a threatened tree take flight, and later in the season only the adult herons in the targeted nest will take flight, with the rest remaining to protect their offspring. A heronry in the Black River wetlands near Seattle was devastated between 2004 and 2010 by the repeated nest predation of a pair of Bald Eagles nicknamed Bonnie and Clyde. Some herons, although not those in Stanley Park, actually locate their rookeries near eagles' nests, in a "devil you know" tradeoff whereby they lose occasional offspring to the resident predator but gain protection from competing eagles.

The crows flew off, and the relative quiet resumed. As I packed my camera to go, I wondered if courtship and nest-building were mostly done for the season and if the herons had begun laying eggs. I looked down, and almost at my feet was an empty eggshell, or half of one. The shell fit neatly into the cup of my hand: oblong, a pale grey-blue, uniform in colour and about the size of a lemon. Not only were the herons laying eggs, at least some of them had hatched!

* * *

In mid-May, about a week after park staff made the "official" announcement that the rookery's chicks had hatched, I returned with my own offspring, and the scene had changed again. This time we smelled the herons before we could see them: wafts of fishy breeze met our noses, but the nests were partially concealed by new leaves in bright yellow-green. Once we got closer, my teenage daughters spied the tufty nests and, using their twin powers, shouted in unison, "Truffula trees!" for the fanciful and ill-fated forest guarded by Dr. Seuss' Lorax.

I am the Lorax
I speak for the trees
Which you seem to be chopping as fast as you please …

The story-book quality of the scene was enhanced by blue sky and a purple carpet of bluebells and bleeding hearts in the fenced-off area under the trees.

Less lovely, the ground was splashed white with droppings, or "splay." What we commonly call bird poop is actually bird urine. Birds have a single opening for reproduction and excretion, and there are no separate exits for urine and feces. Bird poop is the darker solid waste at the centre of the white uric acid paste. Unlike previous visits, a splattering sound on the leaves above gave a warning, and the falling waste was broken up so that the likelihood of a full hit was reduced. Even with the bird-made precipitation reduced to showers, standing below a hundred heron nests is by no means risk-free: a brittle four-foot-long branch grazed my sleeve and shattered at my feet. Someone above must have been doing a little housekeeping.

Discarded shells littered the ground. My daughter pointed out the first, and I seized it with excitement as she and her sister headed off with a blanket in search of unoccupied trees to read under.

In answer to the perennial question about chickens and eggs, or in this case herons and eggs, I usually opt for the smart-ass evolution response: eggs came first; dinosaur eggs, to be specific. Eggs existed for a long time before chickens evolved. But in terms of an individual bird and egg, the answer is found in the coiled oviduct of the female bird. Inside the adult female heron is something of a reproductive assembly line. An egg cell is produced in the ovary and develops a yolk—a sack of protein and fat that will feed the developing heron. The germ cell is fertilized by sperm, either freshly arrived from an act of mating, or from temporary storage at the top of the oviduct. As the egg moves toward the cloaca, the albumen, or egg white, which provides structure and hydration, is added around the yolk and fertilized germ, and then membranes are added. Finally, the calcium carbonate shell is formed over the membranes, and a clutch of two to five eggs is laid, each one to two days apart.

As the hour unfolded, I started to see shell fragments on the ground all around me and began a process of discarding successive partial shells for more and more intact upgrades, a kind of frenzied greed for an obscure currency. At one point, I had shells in the cargo pockets of my shorts, one in each pocket of my shirt, and one that I had to keep setting down, on a fence post or my shoe, as I tried to take pictures.

The smell was strong, like an open tin of cat food at my elbow. But more striking than the smell was the noise, a constant chat-chat-chat, pause, chat-chat-chat, one-two-three; one-two-three; one-two-three-four; one-two-three. I looked around, expecting to see a flock of tiny songbirds—but with dawning wonder I realized this insistent peeping was the sound of *200 heron chicks demanding to be fed!*

Compared with my last trip, the adult herons were much more visible, not hunkered down incubating eggs, but standing on the edges of now-full nests. Activity in the sky was more sparse and more businesslike, no circling flights. Adults announced their arrival and quickly switched places on the nest: one in and one out, with little interaction beyond some adjusting of position. Two adults and two chicks will consume nearly

2,000 calories per day, requiring the adults to forage almost constantly. Both males and females incubate eggs and feed young. Herons have particularly good night-vision, and often the female will hunt during the day and the male at night. Hunting by sight, they grab or stab their prey with long, dagger-like bills. Fish and frogs are their most usual quarry, but they've been known to eat rodents and even smaller birds. When the juveniles are ready to hunt independently, they tend to feed inland, while adults stick to the coast.

During nesting season, herons eat mostly small fish. As I scanned the sky above, I hoped for the chance of seeing an adult make a meal delivery. None of the arriving birds was obviously carrying anything. Birds kept arriving, beaks empty. And then there was one carrying something—a fish? No, a branch. As I watched, it became clear that this heron and its mate were building a nest, or perhaps rebuilding one that had failed. The male flew off, selected additional branches and presented them to his mate, while around them chicks were clacking and crying for food. This pair was more than a month behind.

I never did see a heron carrying a fish. It turns out that herons feed by regurgitation, vomiting food into the nest for the chicks to eat.

On the ride home, my children rolled down the car windows, informing me that I reeked. I realized that my camera strap had crushed the blue shell in my shirt pocket, releasing a cloud of essence-of-rotting-fish about my person. I told them they should be glad I didn't use the heron method of preparing dinner.

* * *

On the 20th of May, I brought a friend but no camera. As we approached the rookery on foot, I stopped our conversation. "Listen," I hissed, and over the traffic and the holiday weekend beach crowds, the insistent crying of the chicks was audible half a block away. As we got nearer, I could see that the bluebells were gone and the grass had grown up about two feet in the week since I'd been here. The only shells I could see were clusters of tiny fragments, the largest about the size of a dime.

The activity level was at a pitch similar to the height of breeding season. Adult herons in the air were flying in every few minutes, trading places with mates perched on the edge of nests or on branches nearby. Despite the constant calling of the chicks, I couldn't see any. The trees were even more greened-in, but from our steep angle below, without any enhanced lenses the chicks were invisible. I thought *maybe* a thick, pointy stick on the side of a nest might be a bill, but it was hardly convincing—even to myself.

My companion, Denzil, and I offered each other the bad directions of two people with almost the same perspective trying to point out the distinguishing characteristics of virtually indistinguishable branches and nests:

"D'you see the big fork there?"

"On the right?"

"Yes, on the right of the tallest tree. Okay, now go up the left fork about two-thirds—"

"Got it!"

"Well not that nest, but two nest-widths over a bit and then down?"

"With the adult on the side?"

"No the nest under that, the adult is on the branch above."

"Now watch the right side of that nest; I thought I saw movement."

Beside us, a pair of photographers with lenses the size of a ballerina's thigh claimed there were chicks at the side of that nest. The most I could see was a play of light and dark in the gaps between the sticks. Then a shadow that could not have been made by the adult perched on the edge of the nest, appeared and disappeared.

It was hard to know what strategy to employ. Should I look where the lenses were pointing? Try to detect responsive movement when an adult flew in to a nest? Keep vigilant focus on the one nest where I had at least seen signs of chicks? Or turn my head, chasing every motion, in a

A SIEGE OF HERONS

perpetual game of catch-up. (Have I mentioned my extensive collection of photographs of branches where birds used to be?)

The movement of adults kept drawing my focus. The pair with the new nest were still building, the male flying in sticks and the female fitting them into an untidy platform.

Finally, to the left of the nest I had been marking, I saw what was unmistakably an open bill, maybe half the size of an adult's, appear and disappear over the edge of the nest next door. Without taking my eyes from the nest, I grabbed Denzil by the arm and tried to pivot him into a position where he could see. As I watched, a spiky, rust-coloured head appeared and disappeared, and I literally jumped up and down, clapping my hands. A little later, a boomerang-shaped wing cleared the edge of the nest. Twice!

I turned my attention back to the nest with the light and dark shapes and was almost instantly rewarded. Like a puppet show viewed from the very bottom of the stage, a pair of small bills appeared and tapped against each other. No head cleared the edge of the nest, but it was definitely sibling interaction.

Baby heron nest-life is a fairly bloodthirsty business. Eagles, Great Horned Owls, and Raccoons prey on eggs and hatchlings, while projectile vomit is the chicks' only self-defense. If food is plentiful and predators few, all chicks will survive, but if there is scarcity, younger siblings may starve to death, be pushed out of the nest, or killed in the nest by older siblings. In a typical clutch of three or four eggs, only one or two chicks survive.

Denzil and I continued to stare up at the nests, moving around the site. After about 40 additional minutes, the wing, the head, and the sibling shadow-play were as exciting as it got. Fearful that my friend might not be quite as enthralled as I, I proposed walking further into the park. But my head was filled with the silhouettes of tufty nests and the gangling grace of herons slowing impossibly to land.

SOURCES AND RESOURCES

Birds Through an Opera Glass

By Florence Augusta Merriam Bailey
University of Virginia, 1899
In an era where naturalists studied birds by shooting and examining them and the slaughter of birds for the millinery trade was at its peak, Bailey promoted watching birds as a suitable activity for young ladies and in doing so set the standard for future field guides. The book contains short essays describing the appearance and behavior of common North American birds and is available online and in various reprints.

Birdwiser

By Chidi Paige
A table-top card game for ages 4 and up with matching cards that teach field markings and actions cards featuring danger from predators and human-authored threats. Developed by Black birder and natural science educator Chidi Paige, the illustrated deck focuses on birds of Eastern North America, so there are species that do not appear in the west.
birdwiser.com

British Columbia Conservation Data Centre

On the provincial government website there is a wealth of information about ecosystems and wildlife in British Columbia and their conservation status.
gov.bc.ca/gov/content/environment/plants-animals-ecosystems/conser-vation-data-centre

COSEWIC Assessment and Update Status Report on the Great Blue Heron *Ardea herodias fannini, fannini* subspecies in Canada

Canadian Wildlife Service, 2008
A comprehensive assessment document on the conservation status of the Pacific Great Blue Heron in Canada. Very detailed, but accessible to the lay reader.

Flying Dinosaurs in the City

By Maria Morlin, 2017

A 55-minute narrated amateur documentary about the challenges and triumphs of the Pacific Great Blue Heron breeding season at the Stanley Park rookery.

youtube.com/watch?v=M9kgGzN4afI

The Great Blue Heron: A Natural History and Ecology of a Seashore Sentinel

By Robert W. Butler

UBC Press, 1999

Research scientist Robert Butler has distilled more than a decade of work into an account of a year of heron life on the British Columbia coast. Illustrated with photographs and intended for general readership, the book includes the bird's ecological significance and the threat of habitat loss due to urbanization.

Great Blue Heron FAQ

By Robyn Worcester

Stanley Park Ecological Society, 2014

A short, clearly laid out, readable document reviewing basic information on Great Blue Herons and the Stanley Park Rookery.

"Keeping Feathers Off Hats—And On Birds"

By Angela Serratore

Smithsonian Magazine, May 15, 2018

The Smithsonian Museum marked the 100th anniversary of the Migratory Bird Act Treaty with an exhibit featuring clothing and accessories made from the feathers and bodies of birds, displayed alongside naturalist J.J. Audubon's paintings of the same birds alive and in flight. Serratore's article highlights the work of early ornithologist Florence Merriam Bailey and looks at fashion, gender, and conservation.

The Lorax

Written and illustrated by Dr. Seuss
HarperCollins, 2012
First published in 1971, this picture book about hope and responsibility
has been in print ever since. A boy in a deforested valley learns from the
Once-ler about how, in his greed, he failed to listen to the Lorax, who
speaks for the trees.

Stanley Park Heron Camera

Visit online in the spring to see live footage of herons at the Stanley Park
Rookery courting, building nests, mating, and raising young. Recorded
footage is on the site year-round.
vancouver.ca/parks-recreation-culture/Heron-cam

**Stanley Park's Secret: The Forgotten Families of
Whoi Whoi, Kanaka Ranch and Brockton Point**

By Jean Barman
Harbour Publishing, 2005
A chronological account of the three main settlements in what would become
Stanley Park. The book covers the displacement of these communities
from the late 1890s to the early 1930s. Themes include oral versus written
traditions, who is considered Indigenous, and ownership of land.

A Colony of Bats

4

The bat (vespertilione), a lowly animal, gets its name from vesper, the evening, when it emerges. It is a winged creature but also a four-footed one, and it has teeth, which you would not usually find in birds. It gives birth like a quadruped, not to eggs but to live young. It flies, but not on wings; it supports itself by making a rowing motion with its skin, and, suspended just as on wings, it darts around. There is one thing which these mean creatures do, however: they cling to each other and hang together from one place looking like a cluster of grapes, and if the last lets go, the whole group disintegrate; it [is] a kind of act of love of a sort which is difficult to find among men.

Aberdeen Bestiary, 13th century

My initial plan for this book was to visit one mass gathering of creatures each month, and spend the time in between learning and writing about them. Turns out, that's not really how animals work. It's not how seasons work; and it's not how writers work, either. My visits to the heronry lasted well into May, but as I planned for subsequent chapters I began to worry that there might not be any more animal gatherings until fall. If you live at a midpoint on a migratory bird flyway, there's just not that much action in the summer; after breeding season, many birds keep a low profile while molting. Although half of this book is about encounters with birds, the summer chapters document gatherings of mammals, insects, amphibians, and fish; we don't see birds again until fall. Thank goodness for the Burrvilla bats.

A couple of years ago, I learned that the prosaically named city of Delta, just south of the Fraser River, is home to one of the largest maternal bat colonies in British Columbia. Knowing that the colony was so nearby, even though I had never visited, was one of the motivators for writing this book.

I have always had a soft spot for bats. As a kid who was pretty terrible at social norms and gender expectations, I felt an affinity for these creatures that seemed to be neither one thing nor another. When I was in Grade 3, my mother sewed me a bat costume from a dyed bed sheet, and although chicken pox, measles, or another of those childhood spotted illnesses kept me from trick-or-treating, the bat wings were a costume-box staple for years. Living in the city, most of my encounters with bats were on camping trips in the summer, making them seem special and exotic. The fact that vampires could turn into bats only enhanced their appeal, and nothing in my adult experience and learning has dampened my enthusiasm for these flying mammals.

In university, an introductory vertebrate zoology course required students to do a literature review on a species native to British Columbia. What this meant was a short but comprehensive essay about the animal's evolutionary relationships, appearance, range, behavior, reproduction, and conservation status, citing *every* published scientific reference to the animal. Points would be deducted for each missed reference. In the pre-internet era, this meant painstaking searches through corridors of tiny-drawered card catalogues, musty stacks of journal abstracts, interlibrary loans of near illegible photocopies, and then a rigorous cross-checking of each article or book's citations. I chose the Townsend's Big-Eared Bat, a 10-centimetre bat with four-centimetre ears. And while I got full marks for the references, I lost points for going on at length about the mechanics of bat copulation and birth (let the reader beware).

Our local bat colony is in the south arm of the Fraser River on an island named for John Sullivan Deas, a Black tinsmith who built the first commercial salmon cannery in the province. Deas Island is better known to many in the province as the location of the rush hour-congested George Massey Tunnel connecting Richmond and Delta. The 300-hectare island of Cottonwoods and wetland is a regional park with a rowing club, walking trails, and relocated historic buildings, including Burrvilla, the elaborate Queen Anne revival home of a prosperous local farming family, the Burrs. In late elementary school, I would rush home for lunch each day to watch their great-nephew Raymond Burr solve crimes as courtroom lawyer Perry Mason, sprinting back to school at the sound of the warning buzzer. Through his career, Burr acted in film noir, thrillers, and monster movies, mostly playing villains, so it seems fitting that on summer nights, 3,000 bats pour from under the peaks and gables of his family's home and are silhouetted against the sky.

We waited at the back of the house, craning our necks. While my partner is remarkably tolerant of the milk crate filled with animal skulls in the dining room and birds' nests on top of the freezer, her appreciation of the more-than-human world tends more towards sunsets, lilacs, and pugs in sweaters, so when Julie consented to come and see the Burrvilla bats, I was astonished.

We had arrived early, so we applied insect repellent, identified the correct gable of the house, and then set off along the slough to kill time. To my delight and Julie's unease, we happened upon a small crow roost. Fifty to 100 crows were flying across the water, weaving between the Cottonwood trunks, and settling in for the night. At Julie's urging, we hastened away from the low-flying crows, checking the time of sunset on our phones and wondering about the difference between astronomical and nautical twilight. (It has to do with how many degrees the centre of the sun is below the horizon, if you were wondering.) Both were approaching, so we applied more mosquito repellent and returned to stand behind the many-windowed house that now serves as the park caretakers' home. Staring up in the drawing darkness, I tried to keep my eyes on the place where the roofline contrasted sharply with the sky: a small gap unobscured by trees or chimneys. There were a few other people walking in the park, but I was surprised that we were alone on the path behind the house. If 3,000 bats were due to arrive any minute, why were we the only ones there? Surely others must be as compelled as I by the promise of bats in the thousands. Was this the wrong spot? The wrong season? The Metro Vancouver Regional Parks website had advertised a bat tour the next night—same time, same place, so I hoped we were right.

The mosquitoes were many and aggressive and, I found out later, not completely deterred by my layers of clothing. Only my hands and face were exposed, but I came home with a dozen bites. Surely there was plenty for the bats to eat. Why weren't they coming?

Then a flicker of motion at the roofline.

Is that a … nope, dragonfly.

I was afraid that if the bats didn't show soon, we wouldn't get to see them at all. The park gate is locked at 10 p.m.; maybe we needed to come back later in the month when the sun would be setting earlier.

It was late July and sunset was at 9:02, a full four hours later than my sojourn at the crow roost in early February. Then, at 9:04, against the empty sky above the house, a single bat appeared. I hadn't seen it leave the house; it was just there, fluttering in the air, and was gone.

One of the things that delights me about bats is their zigzagging flight. A bat in flight looks remarkably like a cheap toy that was ubiquitous in my childhood: no birthday party loot bag or fall fair fishpond was complete without a rubber bat bouncing erratically on an elastic string.

Bats are the only mammals capable of powered flight. Flying squirrels, lemurs, and possums only glide, as do a diverse variety of "flying" fish, frogs, snakes, lizards, rays, and even squid. In my student assignment on Townsend's Big-Eared Bat, I learned about bat wing-structure and the possibility that the two major groups of bats, fruit bats and insectivores, may have evolved flight separately. I became fascinated by the controversies and seeming contradictions in the evolution of flight. At a minimum, flight has evolved three times in vertebrate lineages: in pterosaurs, birds, and bats. In each case a forelimb with the same bones as a human arm, hand, and fingers evolved into a very different wing structure.

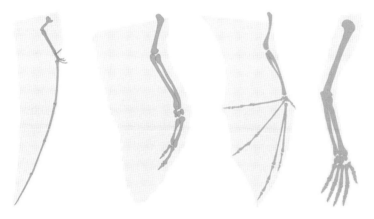

Pterosaurs evolved over 200 million years ago and flew for 150 million years, appearing in the fossil record after dinosaurs but going extinct about the same time. In pterosaur wings, the flight surface is a thin, unsupported membrane with the major bend between the hand and finger bones. Three small fingers protrude from this joint, and the remainder of the wing's leading edge is an elongated pinky finger. Pterosaurs are described as either bat-winged or bird-winged depending on whether the trailing edge of the wing attached to the ankle or torso.

Birds evolved about 50 million years ago. In birds, the major wing joint is at the wrist. The hand is fused and provides some structure, but as you know if you've ever eaten chicken wings, bird wings don't have a lot to them; the flesh and bone is quite limited and it is feathers that provide both structure and flight surface.

In bats, which appeared in the fossil record more or less fully formed about 55 to 65 million years ago, the wing bends at the wrist like a bird's and has a protruding thumb. The flight surface is a membrane, which attaches along the side of the body right down to the ankle and between the legs and tail. The wing is supported by elongated hand and finger bones that extend through it, like the ribs of an umbrella. The scientific name for bats, *Chrioptera,* meaning "hand-wing" in Greek, refers to these structures. The flexible bones and the muscles that control them allow bats to partially fold their wings on the upstroke, creating that distinctive rubber toy flapping pattern and making their flight more energetically efficient than that of birds.

After a minute or two more of hard staring at the sky above the roof, we saw a second bat. It flew out from under the shingles beneath the eaves and was silhouetted for a moment against the light-coloured fascia board. Five minutes later there was another. One at a time, slowly at first, more tiny, dark forms began to emerge from either side of the peaked roof. Then, suddenly, it was as though a tap had been turned on, and bats were pouring out of undetectable openings, each one a tiny flick of motion visible across the lighter wood of the eaves, sharp for a moment against the clear sky, and then gone.

After several minutes of quiet wonder, I became curious. How many bats were we actually seeing? My online research said this was the largest known maternal bat colony in the province, with an estimated population of 3,000. Surely we had seen hundreds of bats, but were we approaching my arbitrary 1,000 mark? I set my phone timer for a minute and counted every bat I could see leave the building: 31! I couldn't watch both sides of the eaves at the same time, and I'm pretty sure I counted some individuals twice as they swooped back in front of the house, but on four repetitions I averaged 29 bats per minute leaving the house. At about 9:50, just before we left the park, the numbers had decreased to about 20 or 21 per minute. If I calculated 25 bats per minute for 40 minutes I could safely say that I had seen 1,000 bats.

What do you call a thousand bats? Fruit bats are often called "flying foxes," but the delightful collective term for foxes is "an earth," which makes an unfortunate choice for flying mammals. An early English word for bat was "flittermouse," although in evolutionary terms, they are more closely related to humans than they are to rats or mice. The quote from the Aberdeen bestiary at the top of the chapter shows that medieval naturalists were interested in the unique physiology of bats and in their collective behavior, but neither Dame Juliana nor her successors list a company term for bats, so we must make do with the prosaic *colony* and content ourselves with the fact that the creatures themselves are substantially more interesting than their names.

For the bat novice, here is a bit of an introduction. There are more than 1,300 known living species of bats, ranging in size from three to 170 centimetres in wingspan, or bumblebee to eagle, and *making up about one-fifth to one-quarter of all mammal species!* There are two main groups of bats: large fruit-eating bats *megachiroptera* and small insect-eating bats *microchrioptera*, (although there is some overlap in size). Fruit bats are active at dawn and dusk and find their food by sight, while insectivores hunt at night using echolocation. There are 19 species of bats in Canada, all insectivores, and 16 of these live in British Columbia.

The Burvilla bats are a mixed colony of Yuma and Little Brown Bats. Little Brown Bats are the most common bat in Canada, distributed over most of the forested regions of the North American continent and feeding primarily on insects with aquatic larvae. Yuma Bats are less forest-specific and more flexible in their feeding habits; they live all over the western part of the continent. These two sparrow-sized bats belong to the genus *Myotis*, "mouse-eared" bats and are so similar in appearance and size that researchers on the Burvilla project distinguish between them using instruments that register the sonic frequency of their cries.

There are two kinds of bat colonies. In the fabulously named "hibernacula," mixed groups of males and females, and sometimes mixed groups of species, spend the winter together in caves, human-built structures, or trees, locations which provide high humidity, stable temperature, and protection from predators like owls, Raccoons, and domestic cats. Then there are maternal roosting colonies like Burvilla, where females, and subsequently their pups, spend spring and summer.

Speaking of pups, given that there so many species of bats, it is not surprising that they have varied and creative sex lives. There are bats that attract mates with pheromones, bats with loud, honking mating cries, monogamous bats, polygamous bats, harem-keeping bats, bats that mate in the air, bats that mate upside down, bats that practice fellatio, and other bats that practice cunnilingus.

Like most insectivores, Yuma and Little Brown Bats participate in a behavior called "swarming." In the fall, large numbers gather at their hibernacula and both male and female bats mate with multiple partners. They copulate hanging upside down or in crevices and cave walls, with the males, who are smaller, mounting females from behind. This period of mating continues until their physiological processes slow for winter and the animals fall into a state of torpor. Little Brown Bats are one of many species that engage in same-sex sexual behavior: alert males will mount and copulate with torpid roosting bats, both male and female.

Insect-eating bats are unusually long-lived for their size. In mammals there is a broad correlation between body size and lifespan—the bigger you are, the longer you live. But insectivorous bats live about three times as long as animals of a similar size. Little Brown Bats live an average of about six to eight years but individuals have been known to live as long as 30 years in the wild. It is thought that the slowing of physiological processes like heart rate, breathing, and metabolism during hibernation may contribute to bats' longevity.

Although these bats mate in the fall, females store the sperm in their bodies through the winter, delaying fertilization until they emerge from hibernation in the spring. In April, female bats begin arriving at Burrvilla, entering through spaces under the roof, some less than a centimetre wide, and clinging to the rafters in the attic. The bats are so small—females weigh about as much as two loonies—that even 3,000 of them do not disrupt life for the caretakers living below. A single pup is gestated for 50 to 60 days, and when the mother is ready to give birth she flips so that her head is pointed up and birth is aided by gravity, with the pup falling into a membrane between her feet. While tiny, the pups are proportionally huge, up to one-third of their mother's body weight, and born able to cling to her nipple or the roof of the colony. A lactating female will leave her pup and go out to hunt, eating as much as her full body weight in insects each night. Returning mothers identify their pups by scent and call. At three weeks, pups can fly independently and begin to wean. Females become sexually mature in their first year, and males in their second. In August, bats begin to leave the roost for their winter homes. While reproductive females spend most of their lives in colonies, males and nonbreeding females roost alone or in much smaller colonies during spring and summer; they are the first to return to the wintering sites.

Above the clearing made by the Burvilla house yard and a small footbridge over a creek was a patch of open sky where we could see the bats against the darkening blue. Most were flying away to the west, higher than the two-storey Burr house, and dispersing into the park. I spent a long time trying to photograph them, long exposures creating a trail of repeating wingbeats. When it got too dark for pictures, we moved from the clearing into the trees, and the experience became quite different. Bats were flying in all directions, lower and much nearer to head level, changing direction, chasing insects among the trees.

"I promised my co-worker that if I touched a bat I would go straight to a doctor," Julie said conversationally, as a bat flew between us on the path. Julie works at a hospital, and only a week before we had learned about the first human case of rabies in our province in over 15 years. A Vancouver Island man had swatted at a bat, made contact, but could see no bite or scratch. He was dead within a month. A moment later, a bat zigzagging above me darted to within a metre of my face, and at the same moment, a leaf brushed my exposed hand. I couldn't stifle my gargled yell. Bats have a bad reputation.

In the late 1990s I used to frequent a second-run dollar movie theatre. Having endured my enthusing over "bat facts," my then best friend and now co-parent, Bruce, asked me to see the film *Bats*. He seemed oddly surprised when I said yes.

In the darkened theatre, the scene opened on a high school–aged boy and girl on a car date in a secluded location near a railway trestle. Their romantic encounter is interrupted by repeated rustling and a flash of out-of-focus wings.

"What was that?"

"It's nothing."

Then, as a train screamed by on the tracks, a swarm of giant bats attacked, and the audience endured 36 seconds of smash-cut screaming, flailing limbs, flapping wings, broken glass, flashing lights, and gore. As the screen turned the red of a distant sunset, a string of hanging letters flipped over to form the word "BATS," and I leaned over to Bruce and whispered, "I thought this was a documentary."

In our semi-hysterical laughter, we missed the introduction of Lou Diamond Phillips as the local sheriff, who, along with a biologist played by Dina Meyer, must save a small Texas town from murderous, hyper-intelligent, genetically modified fruit bats.

Because of their nighttime habits, their status as the only flying mammal, their homes in caves and abandoned buildings, and their association with disease, bats, like other things that are different or unknown, are often misunderstood. So, a little myth-busting is in order. Bats are not blind, and some have excellent vision. Bats do not become entangled in human hair, and although insectivores will fly close to a cloud of insects near a person's head, their echolocation is sensitive enough to detect and avoid objects the width of a human hair. As for vampire bats, there are only three species and all are quite small, only a little larger than the Burrvilla bats, and they all live in Mexico, Central America, and South America. A vampire bat consumes about two tablespoons of blood a day, rarely from humans, and most often from large animals or birds. They do not suck the blood but lap it up, after making an incision with teeth so sharp that people handling bat skulls in labs and museums often sustain cuts.

Many people are afraid that bats carry rabies. For a long time, the prevalence of rabies in bat populations was wildly overestimated because researchers only tested bats that were sick, dead, or behaving erratically. In healthy bat populations, random testing indicates that about 0.5 percent carry rabies, and transmission to humans is extremely rare: fewer than five cases in Canada since 1925. Once an infected person starts showing symptoms, however, rabies is nearly always fatal, so it is still important to treat bats with caution. Do not pick up a dead or sick bat, and if you accidentally come into contact with a bat, consult with a doctor or public health line. Those, like me, who were warned in childhood that exposure to rabies meant 21 needles in the stomach will be pleased to know that for the past several decades, the post-exposure treatment has consisted of four shots, one administered at the site of exposure and three in the arm.

While bats can be disease vectors, Little Brown Bats, especially, are at much greater risk of becoming disease victims. White-nose syndrome is a fungal disease that is devastating bat colonies in eastern Canada and the United States. The fungus attacks hibernating bats and can spread quickly through a colony. It invades and destroys the bats' skin and is named for a white fuzz seen around the muzzle of dead or dying bats. Infected bats will wake up in the foodless winter, use up their stored energy, and starve to death; others die from profound disruption of their tissue systems, and many that survive the winter succumb to an immune response that destroys their own tissue. Approximately 6 million bats have died from the fungus, and it is feared that the Little Brown Bat will be extirpated, or regionally extinct, from much of eastern North America by 2026. The disease has not yet been detected in British Columbia as of 2020, although it has been reported in Washington State since 2016. To monitor for white-nose syndrome and to learn more about bats in the province, researchers at

Community Bat Programs of British Columbia are seeking help from the public: contact them if you have bats living on your property, if you find a dead bat, or if you see a bat out in daytime or winter.

The ways that bats endanger humans are exaggerated at least as much as their helpful qualities are overlooked. Bat guano, or bat shit, contains high concentrations of nitrogen, phosphate, and potassium, key nutrients for the growth of plants. In the 1800s, before a synthetic process for nitrogen fixing was discovered, guano, particularly seabird guano, was such a sought-after commodity for agriculture that it sparked a period of American and British colonization, extraction, and labour exploitation known as the "Guano Era." The Guano Islands Act of 1856 was an early American experiment in neo-colonial expansionism, whereby the United States granted itself permission to annex any "unclaimed" islands containing guano deposits. In the United States during the Civil War, guano from bats was mined from caves for the production of gunpowder.

At tropical latitudes, nectar-eating bats pollinate more than 500 species of flowering plants, including wild and domesticated bananas, cashews, and the Blue Agave, from which Tequila is made. Fruit-eating bats play a key role in the maintenance of species-rich tropical forests by dispersing the seeds that pass through their digestive system in a prolific "seed rain." In the northern hemisphere, insectivorous bats impact human food systems in another way. During the spring and summer months, bats consume between 50 and 100 percent of their body weight in insects each night. As many of these insects feed on human and livestock food-crops, this has a huge impact on agriculture. The importance of insectivorous bats to our food systems is one of the reasons that scientists are so concerned about the spread of white-nose syndrome.

After about 50 minutes with the Burvilla bats, it was nearly time for the park to close. As we walked back to the car in the dark, Julie observed, "I'm amazed that there aren't more bats in the sky." Indeed, if we had not come to Deas Island looking for bats but were simply walking by the Burr house a little after sunset, we would have seen bats feeding over the river but would never have noticed them slipping out from under the roof of the house. Three thousand hand-sized bats dispersed over a 300-acre park are pretty thinly spread.

This brief, and perhaps slightly underwhelming, encounter with the Burvilla bats has some parallels to the spiritual life. We often think and are taught to expect that spiritual experiences are written in capital letters, obvious and recognizable: a Burning Bush or a Shattering Realization that sparks a career or lifestyle change.

Our little water faucet of bats is nothing like the Bracken Caves in Texas, where 20 million Mexican Free-Tailed Bats pour out of the ground into the night sky. It is not even as in-your-face as Powell River's 1,000 California Sea Lions, spreading saliva and stink. But this little local helping of wonder demonstrates a couple of seemingly contradictory truths that, when held together, comprise most of what I know about prayer.

The first is that you can prime yourself for wonder. I had an amazing time on Deas Island and reflecting about it afterwards, because I was already excited about bats. A lifetime of curiosity, learning, and fact-hoarding amplified my experience so that each vague silhouette sparked a thrill of recognition and unfolding back-story. This created-being to created-being relationship is what Pinar and So Sinopoulos-Lloyd, of Queer Nature, call "ecological kinship." Our enthusiasm and deep observation are gifts that we can offer both our creature-kin and ourselves. It can become a lifelong exchange that primes us for ever-deeper levels of connection. I think that prayer, meditation, and other kinds of spiritual practice work in a similar way. They are gifts of attention that help to make us ready: a kind of orientation toward anticipation, so that when that "something" happens we don't miss it.

The second insight is that spiritual practice is often unspectacular. I am a priest, but my spiritual life is not a different life that happens when I put on special clothes or perform certain actions; it is my same old, ordinary life, seen or held with a different kind of attention or reverence. As a younger person I used to worry when I was bored or distracted in church or my experiences of prayer, meditation, and worship didn't produce big feelings. I thought that I must be doing it wrong; that I was not good at prayer, not spiritual, or at least not spiritual enough. In frustrated response, I would rail against what felt like "empty ritual." At other times I would try to convince myself that I had experienced more or different than I really had. I see prayer a bit differently now.

My friend Rose Berger, of the Christian-left *Sojourners Magazine,* once interviewed a lifelong practitioner and spiritual elder on the subject of prayer. After fifty years of prayer, he characterized God as "mostly silent." Reading those words, I felt a deep sense of recognition: much of what I experience as prayer is proximity to profound silence. The early Christians called this sense of divine absence the *via negativa.* Sometimes, the best answer we get to human suffering and anguished questions is a mute scribble of bat wings against the sky.

"All's Quiet on the God Front"

By Rose Berger
Sojourners Magazine, March 2008
A short and compelling article by poet and activist Berger about the experience of the absence of God.

Bat Conservation International

A Texas-based international nonprofit dedicated to the conservation of bats. Their website has a wealth of information and resources.
batcon.org

The Bats of British Columbia

By David W. Nagorsen and R. Mark Brigham
Royal British Columbia Museum, 1993
A comprehensive and detailed guide to the 16 species of bats found in British Columbia. Includes detailed drawings, natural histories and identification keys.

Biological Exuberance: Animal Homosexuality and Natural Diversity

By Bruce Bagemihl
St. Martin's Press, 2000
An illustrated guide to the diversity of non-reproductive sexual behaviour and gender expression in animals. Divided into two parts, the book includes "A Polysexual and Polygendered World" and "A Wondrous Bestiary," profiling 190 species.

British Columbia Black History Awareness Society

An organization dedicated to researching, documenting, and disseminating knowledge of the contributions and achievements of Black people to British Columbia. Their website includes teaching resources including short biographies like that of tinsmith and Fraser River salmon canner John Sullivan Deas.
bcblackhistory.ca

Community Bat Programs of British Columbia

A network of community programs to improve the lives of British Columbia bats through research, education, habitat enhancement, and citizen science.
bcbats.ca

Go Do Some Great Thing: The Black Pioneers of British Columbia

By Crawford Kilian
Harbour Publishing, 2020
First published in 1978, this remains the foundational book on the Black history of British Columbia, telling the history through the lives of prominent individuals.

"In This B.C. Mansion, A Massive Bat Colony Hangs on for Dear Life"

By Adrienne Tanner
Macleans Magazine, July 9, 2019
This short popular article on bat research at Burvilla and the threat of white-nose syndrome appeared about the same time I visited the colony.

Stellaluna

By Janelle Cannon
Harcourt Brace Jovanovich, 1993
A beautifully illustrated picture book tells the sweet story of a fruit bat who is raised by birds. She doesn't look or act like the rest of her nest mates, but by being herself she is able to save them from danger. The back of the book includes two pages of bat facts.

Tagging bats to help save BC bat colonies

By Patrick Burke
Metro Vancouver, 2018
A four minute long video showing biologists tagging bats at Burvilla on Deas Island. The importance of the colony, the risk of White Nose Syndrome, and bat conservation are clearly and succinctly explained.
vimeo.com/231004536

A Knot of Toads

5

Go unto Pharaoh, and say unto him, Thus saith the Lord, Let my people go, that they may serve me. And if thou refuse to let them go, behold, I will smite all thy borders with frogs: And the river shall bring forth frogs abundantly, which shall go up and come into thine house, and into thy bedchamber, and upon thy bed, and into the house of thy servants, and upon thy people, and into thine ovens, and into thy kneadingtroughs: And the frogs shall come up both on thee, and upon thy people, and upon all thy servants.

The Book of Exodus 8:1-4, King James Version

We didn't see tens of thousands. At first we didn't see anything but a temporary road sign proclaiming:

Toad Migration
in progress
local access only

There were three of us, two members of my church community, Lini, Jason, and myself; the six-year-old had just had a meltdown and the teenager, learning that she was to be the only party member under the age of 20, had politely but firmly opted for the company of a distraught six-year-old.

Alerted by a vague social media post warning people to stay off certain roads, I recruited my crew and we headed southwest from Vancouver. About an hour out, the cities of Surrey and Langley meet near the Canada-United States border in a jumble of small farms, large lots, warehouses, RV parks, and smell-the-sawdust-fresh housing developments. I turned the car deliberately onto the forbidden road, a narrow two-laner with little space for parking. We rolled along slowly, windows down, eyes peeled for any sign of hopping. Definitely not "local traffic."

We were looking for Western Toads (*Anaxyrus boreas*), an amphibian found on the west side of the Rocky Mountains all the way from Alaska and Yukon in the north to Baja California in the south. There are two known Western Toad breeding ponds near 18th Avenue in Surrey, and a local biologist had estimated that 60,000 recently hatched toads were leaving the ponds for their terrestrial habitat. I had heard about the August toad migration several years ago at Brooksdale, a nearby Christian conservation center, but I had never managed to see them. The promise of tens of thousands of creatures, biblical numbers, whose nearby pilgrimage lasts only a few days, was deeply compelling to me. They were one of the first species I thought of when I began imagining this book.

Adult Western Toads live in a variety of habitats: meadows, forests, shrub land, and prairie. They hunt small invertebrates, mostly insects, which they cannot swallow but instead *pummel down their throats by repeatedly retracting their eyes!* They are active from dusk to dawn and in daytime they seek out cover to stay hidden and to keep from drying out. In winter they hibernate underground.

Western Toads are communal breeders and exhibit strong site fidelity: every spring all the breeding adults in a population congregate at the same shallow location, usually ponds cut off from streams and the larger predators that live there. Males reach sexual maturity at age three or four and return to the breeding site yearly thereafter. Females do not mature until they are five or six years old and breed every one to three years; thus they range further from where they were hatched and are outnumbered by males at the breeding site. Western Toads practice amplexus for external fertilization, which means that when mating, the male grasps the female with his forelimbs and hangs on, fertilizing the black strings of up to 12,000 eggs after they are released from the female's body. With high mortality and a short life span, many females breed only once in a lifetime, while a few males manage to breed multiple times in a season.

Lest we get too stuck in a gender binary, however, one of the distinguishing characteristics of toads is that both males and females possess a "Bidder's organ." Composed of immature egg cells, it is fundamentally an auxiliary ovary, and in some circumstances, triggered by physical or chemical factors, the males of some species will produce mature eggs. Some other amphibians are similarly flexible, exhibiting what scientists call "sex-reversal." Ten thousand gender anarchists were lurking off the roadside in Surrey, and I couldn't wait to meet them.

Tadpoles take one to three months, depending on temperature, to metamorphose into tiny juvenile toads. These toadlets mass together and migrate a kilometre or more as a group before dispersing into natural areas surrounding their home wetland. Why did the Western Toad cross the road? To get to its adult range.

And it was this migration we were hoping to intercept.

When the internet told us we were driving parallel to one of the hatching ponds, I parked on the gravel shoulder. The ponds were completely concealed behind houses and yards to the east of us. We walked north, scanning the road ahead and listening intently; perhaps the short calls of chickadees and juncos were actually toads emitting the "characteristic chirping distress cry" that I had read about. I find it both sad and unsurprising that we recognize some creatures best by their fear responses.

The road and its gravel margins were conspicuously empty. Lini remarked that she wasn't exactly sure what to look for, as her only experience of toads was reading Kenneth Grahame's *The Wind in the Willows,* where the aristocratic Toad of Toad Hall wrecks motorcars and escapes jail disguised as a washerwoman. All three of us had been arrested in nonviolent direct actions opposed to the Trans Mountain pipeline, an expansion project that threatens to move toxic tar sands bitumen to the coast. So we were rather taken by the notion of lawless toads.

After about 300 metres, the road curved east and changed name; we appeared to be circling the breeding ponds. A dry ditch appeared alongside the road, and we continued to scan the pavement, but the only thing moving was an indecisive Border Collie who warned us off, rushed out to inspect, then greeted us enthusiastically, wagging the back three-fourths of his body as he pranced along, escorting us the length of his property. From the other direction a lone figure appeared, pushing a bike and stopping from time to time to point a long-lensed camera at the ditch. I assumed we must be getting close.

The photographer-cyclist, collie, and our group of three converged at a driveway, and a woman crossed her lawn to ask if we were looking for the toads. She pointed across the street to a line of staked-out black landscape fabric. Entirely missable, at less than half a meter high, it ran perpendicular to the road and disappeared into the high grass in the direction of the pond. The fabric fence created a corridor, guiding the toads to a culvert under the road and into the ditch in front of her yard.

"The other night, when it rained, there were a thousand toads," she said. The householder and the photographer with the bike, both long-time residents of the area, fell into conversation lamenting the recent rise in development and the increase in truck traffic, "There used to be deer and all kinds of wildlife here all the time." While they recalled an epic outdoor wedding attended by one hundred invited guests and thousands of uninvited amphibians, Jason spied a single dime-sized toad hopping along the edge of the empty ditch, its dark shape a high contrast to the yellowish rocks.

"I see one!"

"Where?"

"There, beside the rock."

"The rock? All I see is rocks."

"Oh, wait, I see it, too!"

And with eyes and cameras, the whole group studied the tiny dark brown creature, mostly sitting, occasionally moving in languid hops. After several focused minutes, someone spotted another, and then a third toad in the vegetation at the bottom of the ditch. The more we looked, the more we saw. Three, five, 12, 20, 30. Moving. Still.

We fanned out along the ditches on both sides of the road, kneeling, lying down, peering into moss and gravel at the tiny creatures in seemingly aimless travel. Despite their advertised northward migration, the toads were moving in all directions, including toward the culvert leading back toward the hatching pond. Sources of shade and moisture seemed to be the goal; their tiny bodies are susceptible to dehydration in the heat of the day.

The toads ranged in colour from dark brown through greenish grey, to a leopard-like yellow with dark brown spots. The darker markings were slightly raised from the surface of their backs. Some had a pale stripe down the spine. I learned later that the orangeish oval bumps behind their eyes were parotid glands, which excrete a mild poison to ward off predators.

Parotid glands, dry bumpy skin, and a lack of teeth—who knew that many frogs have teeth in their upper jaw?—are what distinguishes true toads from frogs. Frogs have moist, smooth skin, eyes on the top of their heads, and live near water, while toads are land dwellers with side eyes, and they move more by crawling than hopping. We were not so concerned about scientific accuracy and switched back and forth, calling them frogs and toads interchangeably.

Dame Juliana's *Boke of Seynt Albans* does not include a collective term for toads or frogs, perhaps because they do not often appear together in groups, but more recent collections call a group of toads a *knot* (*knob* or *knab*). The description seems apt, as in the ditch clusters of 10 or more tiny bodies overlapped with what seemed a complete lack of regard for personal space. It was hard to be certain (and especially so when I look back at my photographs) where each individual began and ended, whose legs were whose.

I wondered what it would be like to be a toad, climbing over your companions with no sense that some margin of space should exist between the edges of your body and those of a neighbor. No sense of private parts, no notion that only certain body surfaces are meant for casual touching. "Here I go, coming through, oops, sorry, was that your eye, your belly, your throat? What was that soft thing I stuck my elbow into? Gonna rest here a moment and settle my underside across your eyelids."

I wanted to check out the "toad funnel" on the pond-side of the road. When I looked up before crossing the street, the cyclist had drifted toward the bend in the road and the collie and the neighbor had disappeared entirely.

There wasn't much to the funnel: a tiny wall of fabric running from someone's yard right up to one side of the small concrete culvert. On the other side of the culvert a few feet of the same material channeled at least some of the amphibians to the safer crossing. Many didn't find this route; there were toads in the ditch all along the pond-side of the road. I assumed they had fanned out right and left upon meeting the road and were looking for safe passage. Hundreds of quarter-sized stains on the pavement were all that remained of those that encountered cars. Naturalists from Brooksdale Environmental Centre are working with Langley township to incorporate more durable toad migration tunnels into their future road design.

WILDLIFE CONGREGATIONS

In addition to the perils of the road, natural predators take advantage of this annual moveable feast. As we arrived, a Northern Flicker, a striking looking woodpecker known for hammering on skylights and metal streetlamp housings to warn off potential rivals, was hopping along the side of the ditch, stabbing methodically into the grass. I heard the deep thrumming bass call of an American Bullfrog, a baseball-sized invader from the east that is competitor, predator, and disease vector to the Western Toad. A journalist visiting the culvert two days prior at dusk reported a very bulgy garter snake and a Raccoon family tucking in at the migratory buffet. As we drove away at the end of our visit, a Great Blue Heron squawked and launched itself up from behind the houses in the direction of the ponds. In a perfect example of contrasting reproductive strategies, one of the Great Blue Herons' few, precious, intensely invested-in offspring was feeding on the collateral damage of the Western Toads' thousands.

Against the black fabric of the funnel the toads were easier to see, not nearly as dark as they appeared against the sun-bleached gravel. A little group of about seven, heading backward in the direction of the pond, seemed to infect one another with their urgency, hopping faster and faster. As they moved I realized I was looking at the inspiration for language I had used since childhood. Toads at the back of the group jumped over those ahead of them in a repeating pattern. "It's real-life leapfrog!" I exclaimed. "It looks just like the game." We are so animal in our humanness, but I'd lived 50 years without ever seeing frogs leaping this way. I wondered what other kinds of poverty of language modern city-dwelling humans suffer from, when cats and dogs and pigeons and sparrows are the only creature companions that share our spaces, that our eyes land upon. I wondered what ways our language recalls experiences we no longer have: hawk-eyed, as the crow flies, snail's pace, weasel out, happy as a lark. I have witnessed a hawk looking intensely for prey, tracked a crow's more or less straight-line flight, and marked a snail's slow progress, but I have never seen a weasel extricate itself from a tight place, and I am not familiar enough with a lark's song to know if the sound is joyful.

These questions led me again to appreciative musing on the work and insights of So and Pinar Sinopoulos-Lloyd, of Queer Nature. They have expanded my vocabulary with concepts like *interspecies solidarity, multispecies apocalyptic shepherdcraft, social sculpture, guerilla mysticism, interspecies humility, mythic remediation,* and *ecological co-regulation.* In teaching tracking and stealthcraft, they maintain that consent is vital and that animals and plants can and sometimes do assent to being seen, and allowing themselves to be touched.

And the toads? We did touch them—Lini tapping their noses, Jason and I putting our hands in their paths. Some were clearly indifferent, hopping onto the hand in front of them as they would any other obstacle; maybe there was even grudging consent in pausing to blink and stare, quiet, in a cupped hand. Others deftly evaded us or leaped recklessly from our hands.

I am cautious about attributing trust to creatures, plants, and ecosystems, particularly because I know that with the human track record, especially that of European-descended humans, they ought to mistrust me. But I also know there is something that happens to me in the process of paying attention that has to do with borders and boundaries and my own permeability, even a kind of mutuality with creatures and place. It would have been very easy to drive, cycle, or even walk along this road in the admittedly late stages of this toad migration and see nothing out of the ordinary. But by offering our attention, my companions and I have shifted into a different space.

When I am photographing birds, when I have been called to attention by a bird's cry, a pointing finger, or the memory of having seen something special in this place before, something changes in the quality of my perception. At first I am actively searching with an inner narration that goes something like, "There? There? Is that it? Is it there? What about that?" as I trace the edges of shapes looking for patterns or the disruption of patterns. Then the narration and the specific and pointed way that I am looking changes and my perception seems to broaden. Instead of looking *at* the line of a branch or *for* the silhouette of a toad, I am just noticing. Often I will spot one individual, and as I am studying that one I come to an understanding of *how* to see, and then more seem to emerge from the background. It feels like my attention unfolds away from the goal-oriented tasks that are my default mental backdrop, away from the systemic examination involved in searching, and it spreads out, unfurls into a wordless awareness. It is a shift from "looking for" to seeing—and this, I think, is a kind of spiritual practice.

Having shifted to seeing, it became apparent that among the dozens and dozens of tiny Western Toads were a couple of imposters. Pacific Tree Frogs: the same size, but smooth, shiny-skinned, with a dark bar that extends from snout to shoulder across the eye. The frogs we saw were bright green, but Pacific Tree Frogs can vary from tan to almost black, and individuals can change colour seasonally as their environment changes. Where the toadlets will grow to be up to five inches long, the tree frogs (who don't, as it happens, live in trees) are the smallest amphibians on the West Coast, adult-sized at two inches.

Pacific Tree Frogs are extremely common in approximately the same range as the Western Toad. If you've never seen one of these frogs, and even if you've never visited west of the Rockies, I can almost guarantee that you've heard them. They are also known as Pacific Chorus Frogs or Peepers. The male's call to attract a mate—the iconic "ribbit" can be heard at any time of year, but in early spring, males move toward wetlands and a competitive chorus begins. Because of their abundance in Southern California, the Pacific Tree Frog's high chirping call is the sound that signifies "outdoor nighttime" in a Hollywood sound track, whether the film is set in small-town Texas, Paris or Tokyo. The Internet Movie Database has a list of 199 films that include the sound of the Pacific Tree Frog outside of its range. Western Toads, in contrast, are mostly silent. With the exception of a population in Alberta, sound is not a part of their mating behavior, and none of the toads we encountered made distress calls.

Around midday, a crew of young women in reflective vests with clipboards and an odd rectangle of plastic plumbing tubes about the size of a doormat made their way slowly down the middle of the road. They were interns from Brooksdale Environmental Centre, conducting a survey of live and squashed toads. In addition to their more traditional scientific equipment and the PVC quadrat to isolate a standard unit of area for study, the interns carried putty knives for scraping tiny corpses off the road. They confirmed my identification of the tree frogs and the neighbour's assessment that most of the migration has passed. One young woman remarked that she sees toads in her dreams.

And *that*, I thought, is the reason for this whole project, craning up at herons' nests, swatting at mosquitos behind the Burvilla bat house, scanning the gravel for toads. I wanted to spend a year attending upon local aggregations of creatures, because humans have changed; those of us who are not farmers, fishers, hunters, or meat industry workers probably don't dream about animals much. It is not just that our bodies, our eyes, are lonely for the feel and shape of the creatures who were once our companions and competitors, but our dreams have changed, too. When I was a tree planter, I would dream of thousands of tiny trees—pine, fir and spruce seedlings—spaced a metre apart. Now, when I fall asleep I dream of text and images scrolling upwards on a computer screen.

Amphibians are declining faster than birds and mammals. Due to their bimodal lifestyle, they are affected by changes in water, land, and air. Globally, one-third of amphibian species are threatened and upwards of 100 species have become extinct in recent decades. The people who assess the status of wildlife at risk in this country, the Committee on the Status of Endangered Wildlife in Canada, say that the large numbers of Western Toads near mass breeding sites like these can lead to an "exaggerated impression of abundance." Western Toads are a species of special concern on the national Species at Risk list, due to a combination of disease, habitat loss, and habitat fragmentation.

Western Toads are among the 500 amphibian species that have been adversely affected by a deadly fungal outbreak. In a reversal of the biblical story at the top of the chapter, this is a plague on frogs rather than a plague *of* them. Simon Fraser University aquatic ecologist Wendy Palen calls Chytridomycosis, which causes deterioration of amphibians' skin, "the most deadly pathogen known to science." The virulent chytrid fungus *Batrachochytrium dendrobatidis*, spread by trade in amphibians as pets, is responsible for a wave of 90 presumed extinctions, which peaked in the 1980s.

Amphibians are often part of a complex web of relationships: larvae eat algae that would otherwise choke streams, juveniles (juvenile salamanders are known charmingly as "efts") and adults consume insect species that carry disease, and birds and other predators depend on amphibians for food. The loss of amphibians can be devastating to an ecosystem. The regional impact of Chytridomycosis on Western Toads is impossible to assess, because in British Columbia, study of the disease and study of toad populations have rarely coincided.

Western Toads' susceptibility to fungal disease may be increased by environmental co-stressors, namely increased ultraviolet radiation and chemical contaminants in water. On that residential road in Surrey, we witnessed another of the greatest threats: habitat fragmentation. The old joke is turned sideways. Not: "Why did the amphibian cross the road?" But: "Why did the road cross the toad?" Or, more accurately, its home. All over its range, Western Toad habitat is being destroyed by housing developments, agriculture, and logging and mining industries, or cut apart by roads connected to these developments. Those tiny carcasses flattened by cars or cooked on the pavement are repeated on roads over some thirty degrees of latitude, and more than a million and a half square kilometres.

We knelt and sat and lay on the roadside, gravel and pavement, leaving patterns on our exposed skin. Mostly watching, sometimes disjointedly narrating the toads' progress to one another.

"I love how much of connecting with creatures is just sitting doing nothing."

"I like how they butt-wiggle down into cooler spaces."

"Ah buddy, you're stepping all over your friend's head."

"Look at this leopard-print one go."

"They really do have two means of travel: hopping, and then this four-footed, all-terrain commando crawl."

"They actually have amazing clearance when they crawl—like tiny four-by-fours."

"I think the illustrator had the anatomy down right in the *Wind in the Willows*. I mean, minus the clothes."

"Look at their little noses."

"Look at their bellies, they're almost blue."

"I think we've seen at least 300, maybe four."

"They really don't seem to be bothered by us at all."

"Oh, the green ones really do have blue bellies! I was just humoring you. All the bellies I'd seen before looked like skim milk."

Suddenly, hours had passed and we hurried back to the car and the obligations of the city. That night I dreamed of toads.

SOURCES AND RESOURCES

Amphibians and Reptiles of British Columbia

By Brent M. Matsuda, David M. Green, and Patrick T. Gregory
Royal British Columbia Museum, 2006
A readable handbook that is us useful for amateurs and experts. Well illustrated and comprehensive, it describes the 39 species of reptiles and amphibians living in British Columbia. Author Patrick Gregory was the University of Victoria professor who assigned the literature search on Townsend's Big-Eared Bat.

COSEWIC Assessment and Status Report on the Western Toad Anaxyrus boreas in Canada

Canadian Wildlife Service, 2013
This comprehensive assessment document on the conservation status of the Western Toad is very detailed but accessible to the lay reader.

The Frog Book

By Steve Jenkins and Robin Page
Houghton Mifflin Harcourt, 2019
A beautifully illustrated nonfiction picture book that brings together art and science. The illustrations are intense explorations of form, colour, and pattern, and the text describes some of the amazing adaptations of frogs from all around the world.

The Lost Words: A Spellbook

By Robert MacFarlane, illustrated by Jackie Morris
House of Anansi Press, 2018
A lavishly illustrated book of acrostic poetry, invoking and summoning some of the nature-related words that were excised from the Oxford Junior Dictionary to accommodate terms like blog, broadband, and voice-mail. A love letter to nature and language, from acorn to wren, it is suitable for all ages.

"Meet the Western Toad: 5 Ways to Protect a Species-at-Risk Near You"

Brooksdale Environmental Centre, A Rocha Canada
A simple introduction to this species at risk and steps to take for its continued survival. Spend some more time on the A Rocha website to learn about their other conservation projects and education resources.
arocha.ca/5-ways-to-protect-species-at-risk/

"The Plague Killing Frogs Everywhere is Far Worse than Scientists Thought"

By Carl Zimmer
New York Times, March 28, 2019
A clearly written popular article on the devastating global spread of fungal disease in amphibians.

Queer Nature

Pinar and So Sinopoulos-Lloyd teach nature connection and ancestral skills to Black, Indigenous and People of Colour, LGBTQ2IA+, non-binary people and allies. They also offer writing, workshops and consulting, and are doing excellent and thoughtful thinking about race, indigeneity, and decolonization in a wilderness setting.
queernature.org

The Wind in the Willows

By Kenneth Grahame, illustrated by Arthur Rackham
Metheuen, 1908
This classic children's novel has been in print for over 100 years and has been reinterpreted endlessly in film, theater, and dance. Lessons about an all-male society and rigid class structure require some unpacking, but the book conveys a story of friendship, loyalty, and adventure. It also expresses a deep love of place and fascination with the lives of woodland creatures.

WILDLIFE CONGREGATIONS

An Eclipse of Moths

6

She held the moth to the light. It was nearer brown than yellow, and she remembered having seen some like it in the boxes that afternoon. It was not the one needed to complete the collection, but Elnora might want it, so Mrs. Comstock held on. Then the Almighty was kind, or nature was sufficient, as you look at it, for following the law of its being when disturbed, the moth again threw the spray by which some suppose it attracts its kind, and liberally sprinkled Mrs. Comstock's dress front and arms. From that instant, she became the best moth bait ever invented. Every Polyphemus in range hastened to her, and other fluttering creatures of night followed. The influx came her way. She snatched wildly here and there until she had one in each hand and no place to put them. She could see more coming, and her aching heart, swollen with the strain of long excitement, hurt pitifully. She prayed in broken exclamations that did not always sound reverent, but never was a human soul in more intense earnest.

Geneva Grace (Gene) Stratton-Porter, 1909

Welcome to an unexpected chapter, and probably the chapter with the highest squirm-factor, depending on what gets you going.

In early September, a friend in North Vancouver complained about waking up to huge numbers of moths clinging to the white stucco wall of her carport. The next day, the local news reported an outbreak of Western Hemlock Moths in the watersheds on the north shore of the Burrard Inlet. I polled some friends for places where they were seeing moths, and, with a mental list of likely locations, I headed out around sunset.

Moths are nocturnal and, despite outnumbering butterfly species by about nine to one, they are less well known and much less well-regarded than their diurnal (day-active) relatives. There are exceptions in almost every case, but in general, moths differ from butterflies in the following ways. Moths have fuzzy bodies and rest with their wings to the side, either folded close to their bodies or stretched out like airplane wings. Butterflies have slender, smooth bodies and rest with their wings pressed together above their backs. Male moths' antennae have feathery projections to detect female pheromones; butterflies' are thin, with knobs at the end. Moths tend to have dull coloration, while butterflies are brightly colored. Moths change from larvae to adults in a cocoon made of silk; in butterflies the larva forms a hanging chrysalis. The difference being that when a moth is ready to transform, it builds a little change room around itself, while the extra-creepy butterfly larva actually hardens its skin, liquefies, and reforms its insides, then bursts out *through the wall of its own hardened flesh.*

Human habitation on the north shore of Burrard Inlet is creeping up the edge of the Coastal Mountain range. The District of North Vancouver is characterized by steep valleys, rugged inlets, and residential neighbourhoods that end abruptly in forest. When my kids attended a democratic alternative school in North Van, just a 20-minute drive from our urban core home, a Black Bear stalked one of their classmates on his way to school. With the regular juxtaposition of forest and road, and reports of large numbers in different locations, I expected the moths to be easy to find.

My first stop was Lynn Valley, where I headed towards Rice Lake, a popular worship spot for our forest church. I parked near a coffee shop frequented by hikers and walked down a gravel road, across a footbridge and into the park. Uncharacteristically, I had prepared by bringing a flashlight, but I kept it off, preferring to navigate by natural light. I walked for about 20 minutes, alternately looking down at the trail for tripping hazards and scanning the sky above the trees for moths. Nothing.

Occasionally a pale shape would loom out of the darkness in front of my face, a single moth, or sometimes two, but not the thousands I had been promised. I turned around to try some of the other locations on my list. As I approached the car I spied a moth at housetop level. As I followed it with my eyes, it joined a small cloud of moths fluttering around a streetlight. Others appeared until there were perhaps a dozen insects, a kind of bleached-yellow colour, flying in circles. This was a sight I might have paused and watched if I had happened upon it, but nothing I would have left the house to see.

Both the newspaper article and a North Van friend said there were moths in Lynn Valley, so I tried another route into the park. Towards the end of a residential street, I passed by a small gravel parking lot that was unexpectedly full. Assuming that I had found a group of moth enthusiasts, I left my car by the curb and headed back to the parking area. As I approached, it became clear that this was no random happening of insect admirers. These people were organized. Some were directing traffic in reflective vests, others were walking briskly with clipboards and walkie-talkies; there were porta-potties and a couple of trailers, and deeper in the woods, some very bright lights. Clearly, I had stumbled upon a well-funded field research project gathering data on the population outbreak.

I didn't want to interfere, but I really wanted to see the moths. I hoped these real scientists wouldn't mind being observed by an amateur enthusiast. It is my personal and professional experience, however, that forgiveness is often easier to get than permission, so I crossed the parking area as though I knew what I was doing, nodded curtly to the flaggers, and kept on walking. The gravel road on the other side of the parking lot narrowed to a walking path. Still no moths in sight. The path got darker, but I could hear voices and see some bobbing lights off to the right. When a narrow trail snaked off the main path in that direction I followed, scanning for moths and wondering what exactly the research team was studying. Suddenly there was a shout, and bright light cut through the forest about 20 metres ahead of me. I caught glimpses of a young man and woman staggering through the trees at a run. Before the big light was extinguished I also saw tripods, cables, and camera operators. Apparently I had found a movie shoot, not an entomology field station.

Back in the car, I headed south towards the more densely populated Lower Lonsdale, where a colleague had reported seeing moths outside her high-rise apartment. As I rolled slowly through neighbourhoods that seemed to have moth potential, feeling like a stalker, I saw small clouds of moths hovering around streetlights or illuminated briefly by car headlights, but nothing out of the ordinary, nothing deserving the name *boom*, *outbreak*, or *infestation*.

Discouraged and a little embarrassed, I was thinking about packing it in when I remembered the soccer fields at the Lucas Centre, where my daughters used to go to school. Perhaps the moths would be attracted to the bright lights there, if they were even on.

Many moths are drawn to artificial sources of light: fire, lanterns, vehicle headlights, and, I hoped, the large banks of soccer field lights. The behaviour is called "positive phototaxis" and entomologists are not certain why it occurs. One theory is that these night fliers navigate by large celestial bodies of light, especially the moon, which from a moth's perspective are unmoving in the sky. When approaching a smaller, closer light, the moth keeps its body at a constant angle to the light source, the way it would with the moon, causing it to approach in descending spirals. Another theory is that moths exhibit a dorsal light reaction. They are used to light coming from above and orient their bodies so that their backs (or dorsal surfaces) are to the light. "Like a moth to a flame" implies a sort of doomed attraction, but moths are not dimwitted obsessives, rather, they are responding to a completely novel innovation with a strategy that has served them for millennia.

Light pollution, which affects a quarter of the planet's land surface, is believed to be a significant driver in the global decline of insect populations, attracting predators and disrupting mating patterns, navigation, and circadian rhythms. One third of moths circling a light source will die by exhaustion or predation, and it is speculated that the disruption of moths' nocturnal pollination has resulted in an escalating feedback loop of plant-insect population declines. While some human-caused threats and harms to our planet's co-inhabitants, such as changes in climate, loss of habitat, and the introduction of new competitors and predators, mimic changes that happen over ecological time and may then be within species' and ecosystems' adaptive "playbook," the way that artificial light changes day-length is unprecedented.

The good news is that, unlike habitat loss, chemical pollution, and the introduction of parasites, pathogens, and competitors, light pollution is relatively easy to prevent and requires no "cleanup." Researchers suggest that national light reduction targets and more strategic use of light at night could have significant positive impacts for declining insect populations.

I pointed my car west and then north along McKay Creek, the same route that bear and student had taken several years before. Driving up the hill, I could see that the soccer field lights were still on and some moths were gathered around them; my evening had not been a complete waste. As I walked from my car, the extent of what I was seeing became apparent. The air was full of flying insects right from ground level until they disappeared out of sight. Hundreds of tiny moths circled around the huge light stands that illuminated two adjoining fields. Bright white reflected off their wings, but the cloud of bodies was so dense I could stare straight into the normally blinding floodlights. A group of moths is called an *eclipse*, a recent clever name, rather than an ancient one. The only insect group named in Dame Juliana's "boke" is a swarm of bees; since then, groups of insects have been referred to as *swarms* for those on the wing and *colonies* for groups on the ground. Other recent names include a *whisper* or a *kaleidoscope* of moths. A whisper implies subtlety, which the enormous congregation in North Vancouver lacked, and kaleidoscope is a term shared with, and in my opinion better suited to, butterflies, with their brighter colours. This was clearly an eclipse.

The moths belong to a group called Looper Moths, named for their larvae's locomotion. With tiny limbs at the front and back, a caterpillar moves by stretching its front legs forward and then hitching its back legs close behind them, forming a loop with its body. "Inchworm" is the more familiar name. For no reason that I have discovered, an alternative name for the Hemlock Looper Moth is the evocative Mournful Thorn. If we slip for a moment from entomology (the study of insects) to etymology (the origin of words), moths and butterflies make up the vast order Lepidoptera, named for their scaled wings. Their family name is Geometridae, which I had assumed was for the geometric patterns on their wings. In fact, the Greek root words mean earth and measure, referring to the way their larvae cover the ground. I am delighted to think of both inchworms and my least-hated mathematics class as measuring the earth!

Looking up at the moths was like standing in a snow globe. With so many flying above me at different levels, the sky took on a three-dimensional quality that I am not usually aware of, and I experienced a kind of vertigo, as though I too might lift off into the night sky. Some of the photos from my phone resemble pictures of the Milky Way: thousands of tiny specks of light. In others, the long exposures make the moths appear as a repeating trail of wing beats.

Unlike Monarch Butterflies or Hummingbird Hawk Moths, which migrate long distances, Hemlock Moths are weak fliers. Their relatively short-lived adult phase is focused on reproduction. As noted in the chapter on bats, the evolution of flight in vertebrates involved the adaptation of the forelimbs: pterosaurs, birds, and bats in essence traded their front legs for wings. Popular images of flying creatures—the monkeys in *The Wizard of*

Oz, winged horses like Pegasus, or Rainbow Dash of the *My Little Pony* franchise, the ox and lion of biblical prophet Ezekiel's vision—where bird wings have been grafted on to an existing quadruped, fill me with unreasonable rage because they violate this evolutionary principle and because the wings are proportionally too small to support bodies that have none of the requisite adaptations (hollow bones, lack of teeth, concentrated urine, aerodynamic form) for flight. It has been quipped that insects and angels are the only creatures that have not exchanged limbs for wings. On angels I cannot comment, but insects evolved wings about 400 million years ago from extensions of their body walls. And in an evolutionary interplay with terrestrial plants, they changed the face of the planet.

Near the top of the light stands, resting moths overlapped like shingles or scales. At my eye level glimpses of the metal light stand were visible between their bodies, and closer to the ground they were still more sparsely distributed. The surface of the playing field was covered with moths, and although I tried to avoid it, it was impossible not to step on them. On the west side of the soccer field is a forested park that runs along the creek. Looking up, I realized that every branch of every tree surrounding the field was weighted down with moths like some bizarre foliage. Two or three metres deeper into the forest, the trees were less densely covered.

My wonder verged on horror, and it was hard to fathom what I was seeing. Clearly there were thousands of moths, but how many thousands? I tried to count the number of moths on a branch, then multiply that branch by a tree and the trees by the length of the soccer field, and so on. When that calculation failed abjectly, I paced out one square metre and counted 15 moths on the ground. Several repetitions, both closer to the lights and further away, averaged 14 moths per square metre, which I planned to multiply by the area of a standard field.

Apparently one of the aspects of the "Beautiful Game" is that the field, or pitch, is not a regulation size but falls within a broad range. Later, I found an aerial photograph to determine the size of the fields and calculated that there had been just under 140,000 moths on the ground alone!

They were a ghostly greyish white in colour, with bodies like tiny hand-rolled cigarettes. A little wider than a quarter, they were shaped like an arrowhead or a chevron and rested with their wings slightly tented. Across the wings were two parallel dark grey lines, scalloped like a child's drawing of ocean waves. But the moths I had seen in Lynn Valley and those pictured in the news, while they were the same size, shape, and pattern, were gold in colour, with brown stripes. It turns out that our outbreak included two different species belonging to the same subfamily. The yellow-brown Western Hemlock Looper Moths are a broadly distributed North American species whose larvae feed on Hemlock and associated trees. These greyish white Phantom Loopers are found only on the West Coast, and their diet is restricted to conifers.

A Looper Moth outbreak can be devastating. In Eastern Canada, several million hectares of conifer forest have been destroyed by the Western Hemlock Looper. Population booms occur sporadically and last for about three years from outbreak to collapse. The Western Hemlock Looper has been studied more than the Phantom Looper: its one-year lifecycle takes place in a long, vertical oval between the forest floor and the tree canopy. Hemlock Loopers prefer mature or old-growth stands of Hemlock along valley bottoms, but will also live on and consume cedar, fir, and understory vegetation.

Moths have four life stages. In May and June, when juvenile Great Blue Herons are learning to fly and female Yuma and Little Brown Bats are returning to Deas Island, Looper Moth larvae emerge from grey-brown pinhead-sized eggs hidden singly or in clusters in tree bark, moss, or the forest floor. The grey and black inchworms go through five moults, shedding their exoskeletons as they increase in size and move towards the tops of their host trees. The stages between moults but prior to sexual maturity are called *instars*. Unlike Eric Carle's *Very Hungry Caterpillar,* which eats a worm-sized hole through each of its dietary choices, leaving them relatively intact, Looper larvae are destructive feeders, consuming a small portion of each conifer needle but often clipping it from the tree in doing so. A Hemlock that loses 80 percent of its crown this way will die; trees with less crown-loss will also die if the outbreak coincides with a drought, and trees that do survive are stunted by this "topkill." During the month of July, the larvae are at their most voracious, and although the ground below can be littered with discarded needles and insect feces, called "frass," an outbreak often goes unnoticed until the moths appear. In late August or early September the final instars, three centimetres long and spotted greenish brown, descend from the tops of trees on long silk threads spun from their mouths. They pupate in similar locations to where they hatched—bark, moss, and forest floor—transforming from larvae to adults over 10 to 14 days. Moths emerge and females emit pheromones that attract males. Over a period of weeks they mate, lay eggs, and die. The eggs overwinter and the cycle resumes in spring.

After three years, a moth outbreak will collapse through the interaction of a number of factors: disease, predators, parasites, and the carrying capacity of the environment. One significant and fantastically gruesome factor in their decline is nuclear polyhedrosis, a naturally occurring viral infection that can spread rapidly through densely clustered populations. Commonly known as "caterpillar wilt" or "treetop disease," the virus causes infected larvae climb to the top of a tree, where they liquefy internally, explode, and rain virus particles down onto their fellows.

The Western Hemlock Looper is one of the most destructive defoliators in the province. Population outbreaks begin with conditions that favour high larval survival rates. In hot, dry summers, Hemlock foliage is more delicate and thus vulnerable to hungry larvae. Forestry scientists speculate that with rising temperatures and more frequent droughts due to climate change, outbreaks may increase in this region.

Back on the soccer field, the moths were mostly disinclined to land on me, for which I was grateful. They seemed to want a stationary surface, and though I was walking through clouds of them, very few settled on my clothing, 12 or 15 at most. When I realized that a moth had landed on my finger, I held up my hand to watch its progress across my skin. Its touch was so light that until it stirred the tiny hairs on the back of my hand I could not feel its presence at all.

After about 90 minutes that consisted mostly of staring about in wonder and ineffective attempts at counting and multiplication, I was ready to leave. As I approached the car, I brushed off my hair and my clothing, reaching around to make sure that all the parts I couldn't see were moth-free. Only when the doors were closed and I was seated in the driver's seat did I shudder, imagining I could feel the ghostly touch of 10,000 tiny feet.

These are not the only insect ghosts that haunt me. My childhood was full of bugs. On summer holidays to Alberta, my brother and I would fight over who got to squeegee smashed carcasses off the windshield and grill of the van. I remember vacant lots full of whirring grasshoppers, annual kitchen invasions by ants, walking down the middle of the road to avoid tiny green inchworms on threads, tent caterpillar infestations when every tree seemed to have at least a couple of webbed box-kites filled with hairy, writhing worms, and swarms of blackflies and mosquitoes on camping trips and later planting trees. But now? Not so many.

Entomologists have coined the phrase "windshield phenomenon" to describe the dawning awareness of this absence, and it has sparked recent studies documenting a shocking global decline in insect populations. Some have even called this an insect apocalypse and warn that because of their key roles as pollinators and detritivores (consuming dead organic matter), and their place at the base of many food webs, the dramatic loss of insects could lead to catastrophic collapse of ecosystems: a kind of obliteration from the bottom called "trophic cascade."

When we think of large groups of animals, insects are kind of archetypal, a phenomenon that appears and then disappears. Plagues of insects were a stereotypical curse in the ancient Near East. In the book of Exodus, Moses visits three insect "signs" upon the tyrant Pharaoh: biting insects, a mixed swarm, and locusts. Locusts are mentioned in the *Illiad* and the Qu'ran, and they were painted on Egyptian tombs. Locusts are the swarming phase of a few species of normally solitary, short-horned grasshoppers. Outbreaks can number in the billions and devastate millions of hectares of cultivated land. There are no extant locust species in North America, but in 1874, British Columbia was at the northwestern periphery of a devastating plague of the now-extinct Rocky Mountain Locusts, which swept all the way to Texas. In places they would block the sun for up to six hours, destroying crops, clogging wells, and eating even the paint off of buildings. While the Entomological Society of British Columbia records a major locust infestation of Red Legged and Migratory Grasshoppers in the Okanagan in 1915, the last living Rocky Mountain Locust was collected in Manitoba in 1902. By various measures, the Rocky Mountain Locust plague was the largest mass of insects in recorded history, and yet within decades there were none.

Thinking about locusts and Looper Moths highlights some of the contradictions, or at least contrasts, that we face in trying to make sense of what is happening in this human-dominated Anthropocene era: presence and absence; collective and individual; anecdote and evidence; past, present, and future. While perhaps a million moths created a blizzard of bodies on the soccer field, a few blocks away I could find almost none. Each individual was about as substantial as a scrap of torn paper, a blowing feather, but together they form a teeming, destructive mass that can devastate a forest, unnoticed until the damage is done.

In popular use, the word "apocalypse" signifies the end of the world or at minimum a catastrophe, but that is not how theologians use the world. Apocalypse as a biblical genre is exactly what the final book of the Bible promises, a Revelation. The Greek word *apocalypsis* literally means *drawing back the veil*, or figuratively revealing what is already present but hidden. So in this sense, the discovery of insect population declines is a true apocalypse; it is a revelation.

For five, or perhaps 10 years, herbalists, organic farmers, and environmentalists in my circles have been lamenting the global decline in bees: creating hydration stations for the garden, refusing to mow their lawns, and sharing photos of workers in China pollinating apple orchards by hand. Recent studies have shown that many more insects are in trouble. Globally, insects are diminishing in numbers of species, in numbers of individuals, and in geographic range. Although there is a wealth of scientific literature on beetle penises, there is a dearth of long-term quantitative data on insect populations. Even skeptical re-examinations of existing data, however, concede that 40 percent of insect species are experiencing population declines of between 0.9 and 2.5 percent annually, and that land insects, especially those that fly, have been particularly hard-hit. While I twirled like a Hallmark Christmas movie protagonist in a blizzard of moths, the magnitude of changes to insect populations has been devastating ecosystems in ways that cannot help but impact human populations as well.

Predictions of a world without insects are exaggerated, in the sense that this is a future that humans would not survive to see. David Yeates, director of the Australian National Insect Collection, put it this way: "Insects will likely feed on the last vertebrate carcass on the planet." Remember the quote in the first chapter from evolutionary biologist J.B.S. Haldane about God's fondness for beetles? Moths and butterflies alone make up 10 percent of the named animal species on earth. With 900,000 named, insects make up 80 percent of known animal species and have the greatest biomass of terrestrial animals. Insects are both specialists and generalists; they are fast adapters with short generations, so certainly some will survive this great decline even if some mammal species, our own included, do not. But like Gene Stratton-Porter, quoted above, whether that represents "the goodness of the Almighty or the sufficiency of nature," I cannot tell.

The Curious World of Bugs: The Bugman's Guide to the Mysterious and Remarkable World of Things That Crawl

By Daniel Marlos
Perigree, 2010
Illustrated with vintage drawings, this is an enthusiastic and informative resource that includes history, ecology, and entomology. Intended for the curious amateur, the reading level is suitable for older children and adults.

"1874: The Year of the Locust"

By Chuck Lyons
HistoryNet LLC, 2012
An engaging online article describing the Rocky Mountain Locust plague of 1874, found on the website on HistoryNet, a publisher of popular United States history magazines.

Girl of the Limberlost

By Gene Stratton-Porter
Grosset and Dunlap, 1909
Indiana author, naturalist, and nature photographer Gene (Geneva Grace) Stratton-Porter tells the story of a love, poverty, family trauma, and a girl coming of age. In swampland being consumed by logging, oil extraction, and agriculture, the protagonist finds solace and resources for negotiating these complex realities in education, music, and the study of natural science. There have been several film adaptations and the novel is currently available as an e-book.

"The Insect Apocalypse is Here: What Does it Mean for the Rest of Life on Earth?"

By Brooke Jarvis
New York Times Magazine, November 27, 2018
This epic article begins with an in-depth examination of the global decline in insect populations before examining the chilling phenomenon of defaunation, the loss of animal populations and species.

"Insect Evolution: The Origin of Wings"

By Andrew Ross
Current Biology, vol. 27, no. 3, 2017, pp. 113-115.
This short, scholarly, but not too technical article reviews the evolution of wings in insects.

"Insects are the Great Survivors in Evolution: New Study"

By David Yeates
The Conversation, November 6, 2014
A clear and comprehensible article for generalist readers, on new research into insect evolution by the director of the Australian National Insect Collection, published in a Canadian online academic news source.

"Is the Insect Apocalypse Really Upon Us?"

By Ed Yong
The Atlantic, February 19, 2019
A short article responding to Brooke Jarvis' dire "Insect Apocalypse" article. It concludes that while insects are diverse, resilient, and understudied, both research and action are needed for best conservation practices.

"Light Pollution is Key 'Bringer of Insect Apocalypse'"

By Damian Carrington
The Guardian, November 22, 2019
This short popular article is a specific response to Brooke Jarvis' "Insect Apocalypse" article. It describes the ways that light pollution harms insect populations and the ways that harm can be reduced.

"Moth Population Takes Flight in North Van"

By Jeremy Shepherd
North Shore News, September 10, 2019
A short account of the 2019 Looper Moth population boom, including interviews with local forest scientists, published in a local North Vancouver newspaper.

"Outbreak of Hemlock Looper Moth Hits North Shore, Metro Watersheds"

By Tiffany Crawford
Vancouver Sun, September 11, 2019
A newspaper exploration of the causes and impacts of the 2019 Looper Moth outbreak, with emphasis on forestry and climate change.

The Very Hungry Caterpillar

Written and illustrated by Eric Carle
World Publishing Company, 1969
Almost as old as I am, this beloved picture book tells the story of a caterpillar that emerges from a tiny egg and eats its way through the days of a week and a variety of foods before forming a chrysalis and becoming a butterfly. Currently available from Philomel, the book has had more than one publisher and the story has been retold in a variety of media.

Western Hemlock Looper *Lambdina fiscellaria lugubrosa*

By Kim Mellen-McLean et al.
USDA Forest Service, 2017
A succinct article on the life of the Western Hemlock Looper as it pertains to forestry published in a US Forest Service online advisory tool on decaying wood.
apps.fs.usda.gov/r6_decaid/views/western_hemlock_looper.html

What's That Bug?

A labour of love by Daniel "the Bugman" Marlos, author of *The Curious World of Bugs*. This is an amazing and entertaining online resource where insect enthusiasts can send in photos of bugs for identification. An excess of content pertaining to sex and carnage is undergirded by an awareness of the fragility and interconnectedness of life on our planet.
whatsthatbug.com

WILDLIFE CONGREGATIONS

A Run of Salmon

7

If the [passenger] pigeons plagued us by their abundance, the salmon gave us even more trouble. So large a quantity of them enters into this river that at night one is unable to sleep, so great is the noise they make in falling upon the water after having thrown themselves into the air.

Nicolas Denys, 1672

Living on the West Coast, it can sometimes feel like half the year is a single season called "the long grey" that starts in mid-October and ends sometime in March. Growing up, brightly coloured fall leaves were more likely to be laminated illustrations stapled to a corkboard than anything I knew from experience. Autumn leaves were slick, wet, and brown, the air was damp, and the skies overcast. But the day we went to see the salmon was bright, crisp, and full of colour—everything curriculum developers from the Great Lakes bioregion told us fall was supposed to be. Orange deciduous trees were like flames licking up the green hillside; farther away, snowy peaks stood out sharply against a bright blue sky, and beside the road, field after field of blueberry bushes glowed a vivid red.

The sky was full of raptors: more Red-tailed Hawks than I could count, Harriers, a few Turkey Vultures, and plenty of Bald Eagles: one kept pace with the car for several minutes, flying over the Nicomen Slough as we drove beside it.

In mid-October, our wilderness church hosted a group of 10 students from Villanova University on an immersion trip. They had come to learn about how faith communities can support grassroots environmental justice movements. I wanted them to experience first-hand some of the species and ecological forces of the bioregion, so different from their homes in the eastern United States. We were headed to Weaver Creek, a tiny feeder stream to the lower Fraser's largest tributary, the Harrison River. The Fraser River basin drains about one-quarter of the province of British Columbia and is the greatest source of Pacific Salmon in the world. Witnessing a salmon run was a fantastic opportunity for the students; salmon are key to the ecology, culture, and economics of this region, and the peak of this brief and most spectacular phase of their lifecycle happened to coincide with the students' visit.

Their importance to the economy and ecology of the province means that no child in British Columbia gets to high school without studying the lifecycle of the Pacific Salmon. Classrooms have posters on the wall. Field trips to hatcheries and spawning streams, and the opportunity to raise and then release a tank of tiny salmon in the classroom were educational staples that I assumed to be universal until a friend raised in Ontario complained about British Columbians' salmon-smugness—our assumption that salmon biology and morphology are commonly held baseline knowledge.

So for Caitlin, and anyone else who is fuzzy on the details: a review. Pacific Salmon are "anadromous," meaning that they are born and reproduce in freshwater but live their adult lives in the ocean, and "semelparous," meaning that they mobilize all their resources for a single, epic reproductive episode at the end of their lives. The generalized Pacific Salmon lifecycle looks like this.

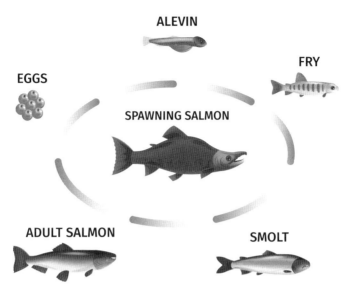

ALEVIN

FRY

EGGS

SPAWNING SALMON

ADULT SALMON

SMOLT

In gravel beds along streams, rivers, and in some cases, lakes, pea-sized salmon eggs develop over the winter. In early spring, the embryo requires more oxygen than can permeate the egg, and it emerges as a gilled alevin. Familiar to the elementary school naturalist, alevins are seldom seen in the wild: these tiny fish remain in the gravel for four to six weeks, feeding on the yolk sac attached to their bellies. When the yolk sac has been consumed, they swim to the surface at night, absorb enough oxygen to fill their swim bladders, and become fry. Fry require a healthy stream bed, where they grow on a diet of insects, larvae, worms, and food particles in the fresh water. Dark vertical stripes provide camouflage from their many predators: snakes, birds, and larger fish, including other salmon. As the finger-length fish move towards river estuaries, their bodies change externally, developing shiny scales, and internally, so that their organs can regulate salt. These silvery smolts enter the ocean, traveling together for protection. As they mature into adults, they disperse broadly for a period of years, feeding on plankton, larval crab and shrimp, and smaller fish. Sexually mature adults return to fresh water, stop eating, and concentrate all their physical resources on reproduction. On an arduous journey upstream, they undergo changes in colour and form. Using a combination of genetic coding, celestial navigation, electromagnetic current, and an incredible sense of smell, they return to the place where they first hatched. They find mates, release eggs or sperm, bury them in the gravel, and die. And the cycle begins again.

Five species of Pacific Salmon live in British Columbia: Chinook, Chum, Pink, Sockeye, and Coho. They are large, torpedo-shaped silver fish with red-pink flesh, weighing between two and fourteen kilograms and measuring from one-third to nearly a metre long. All are members of the genus *Oncorhynchus,* which also includes two species of opportunistically ocean-going trout, and the much smaller Kokanee Salmon, a land-locked form of Sockeye. The generalized lifecycle diagram that adorns countless classroom walls and park interpretive stations is a necessary simplification. It neglects differences between these species, the ways that diverse populations are highly adapted to their habitat, the relative lengths of each phase of life, and human interventions in the process. This chapter will fill in some of those gaps.

The Villanova University students were staying at the Brooksdale ecological centre, where the toad-counters were based. Their first encounter with spawning salmon happened two days before our trip to Weaver Creek. We had spent the morning making a salve with Gitxan and Nisga'a herbalist Leona Brown and went out after lunch to identify medicinal plants, poke at owl pellets, and walk by a short stretch of the 30-kilometre-long Little Campbell River (Tat-a-lu in the language of the Semiahmoo First Nation). Just the week before, I had seen a pair of salmon struggling to get past the resident Beavers' dam and I was hoping the students would have a chance to see them up close.

I arrived at the little river at the head of a line of students and was disappointed to see nothing swimming in the water. As I scanned the surface of the water for dorsal fins, I spied a dead salmon on the far shore that looked like it had been dragged ashore and partially eaten by a River Otter or a Mink. Intent on finding live fish, I continued along the bank.

When nobody joined me, I turned back to find that Leona had taken off her shoes, waded across the little river, and picked up the salmon. The students stood rapt in a circle around her as she held up the fish longer than her arm, blood and scales on her hands, showing them the gills, telling them what an honour it was to get to hold it.

At Weaver Creek, we hoped to see hundreds of salmon. The channel had been built in 1965 to extend and enhance the spawning habitat for Sockeye, a small, abundant, and commercially important salmon. Branching off from the creek itself are three kilometres of groomed stream bed in a folded pattern that winds up a gently inclined lawn, ending with a grated drain. A stable flow of water, regulated for temperature and volume, and a bed of uniformly sized rocks provide a consistent environment for spawners, eggs, and alevins.

We parked in a gravel lot with 50 other cars and entered a nondescript park behind a chain-link fence. There were a few picnic tables off to the side, and a roofed sign showing the ubiquitous salmon lifecycle diagram and pictures of different species. As we followed other patrons across the neatly mown lawn towards a treed area, it became apparent that all the action was happening in the water.

I grew up in Victoria, with an annual pilgrimage in November to Goldstream Park to see the Chum salmon spawn. That palette was misty greens, grey, and brown seen through falling rain, so I was unprepared for the vibrant Sockeye. I had truly imagined that those bright red and green images of salmon jumping over rocks were colour-enhanced for tourists and wildlife magazines. But here were hundreds of fish, all pointed upstream, fighting, splashing, and circling each other, with red bodies and green heads and tails as bright and gaudy as cheap Christmas ornaments.

Although the facility was built for salmon, it was clearly designed for humans as well. Evenly spaced trees had been planted beside the channel, and there was no undergrowth so that visitors could stand right next to the water and view salmon at their feet. While the students dispersed through the park, exclaiming, pointing, thrusting expensive phones into the water to take photographs, I stopped trying to be a good host and lost myself in all that I was seeing. As with the herons in April, there was so much going on that my eye was drawn from scene to scene: splashing water, a flash of colour, one fish driving another away from a choice location, a single floating egg, a bat that shouldn't be out in the daylight fluttering purple between the shadows of the trees, an American Dipper bobbing below the water, hunting eggs.

At first I simply gloried in the overwhelm. Part of what I came for, and the reason for writing this book, was to experience the wild up close and personal, roaring in my face, or in this case splashing and thrashing at my feet. The water churned with salmon vying for position, sidling up close to potential mates, chasing off rivals. Darting, biting, digging. Their colours were garish and their shapes almost grotesque.

While Sockeye were the most noticeable, there were grey-green Chum in the water as well. Both species exhibit sexual dimorphism when sexually mature. In Sockeye, the male's body becomes deeper; it grows a pronounced hump between head dorsal fin, and the snout becomes long and hooked. The female converts most of her body weight to gonads. Both male and female Sockeye change from silver to dramatic red and green. In Chum, the changes are subtler: males also have a hooked jaw and increased body depth but no hump, they grow large teeth and have vertical bruise-coloured markings, like purple and green flames, on their sides. The females change from silver to purple and green, but with a thick, dark horizontal line along their sides. Males and females of both species showed signs of injury and decay—tattered fins, missing eyes, scrapes, and gouges.

The Department of Fisheries and Oceans says that in recent years the annual count for adult salmon at Weaver Creek has been as high as 100,000, and the channel has the capacity to hold nearly half that number at one time. So how many salmon were we seeing? The students' best underwater photograph showed a dozen fish in an area roughly two metres by two metres. An imaginary line across the six-metre channel would touch 12 to 15 individuals. In the first 100-metre fold of the channel there were easily 300 fish. Further downstream, closer to the unenhanced creek, they were a little more widely dispersed, but certainly we were seeing thousands, perhaps tens of thousands.

Artificial rapids, metal grates at a bit of an incline, crossed the channel at several places. Some salmon would slowly rise up and over these, propelled by strong, determined churning of their tails; others would take a run at it and make spectacular jumps, leaping clear of the water. A migrating salmon can jump higher than two metres to climb a waterfall or clear other obstacles.

In some places, the water was perhaps three salmon deep, but mostly it was shallow enough that fish swam along the bottom with their dorsal fins and the tops of their tails out of the water. When I learned that salmon make nests and lay their eggs in gravel, I imagined the sharp-edged, almond-sized rocks of a rural road. But in the spawning channel females were turning on their sides and using their tails to shovel up rounded rocks about the size of my fist. I was impressed by their strength.

I wanted the students to love what I love, to be amazed at the beauty of the salmon, their powerful drive for survival, their sheer numbers and their special place in a complex web of relationships. I kept trying to point out mating behaviors and explain what they were seeing. But for many of them, the lasting impression and the most discussed aspect of the trip was the truck that drove slowly between the curves of the channel while workers heaved salmon carcasses into the back with pitchforks, each one landing with a wet and fleshy thump.

This removal of unsightly and smelly dead fish to make spawning palatable to tourists has discouraged the other-than-human visitors typical at spawning sites: scavengers. Thousands of living salmon struggling upstream to mate means thousands of salmon carcasses clogging the water and littering the shore—a feasting ground for gulls, Great Blue Herons, Bald Eagles, River Otters, Marten, Crows, Ravens, smaller fish, and invertebrates in the stream. A Washington State study documented over 150 animal species partially or wholly dependent on salmon for survival. In years when salmon are abundant, bears carry literally tons of bones, guts, scales, and partial carcasses into forests, moving nutrients through the ecosystem. Some researchers are investigating the importance of salmon urine in distributing nitrogen. These impacts, called the salmon "shadow" or "signature," spread out from stream and river banks and are detectable in nutrients incorporated into the bodies of insects, songbirds, and, most dramatically, trees.

Salmon lifecycle diagrams can give the impression that every egg becomes a spawner, but the salmon life history can also be shown as a pyramid with each level representing relative numbers of eggs, alevins, fry and so on. A female salmon lays 2,000 to 5,000 thousand eggs, depending on size and species. In the wild, perhaps 15 percent of these eggs become alevins the rest are swept away by the current, eaten by birds or fish, or suffocated by silt. Fry can fall prey to river predators or be swept to the ocean before they are developmentally ready. In the ocean, salmon are eaten by other fish and marine mammals, including California Sea Lions and Orca. Each resident Orca in the Salish Sea requires 18 to 25 adult salmon per day to maintain its weight. In fresh water returning salmon are prey to Black Bears and Grizzlies, Wolves, Bald Eagles, and others. Weakened by the rigors of migration, many die before they are able to spawn.

For a population to remain stable, on average two of each female's eggs would need to survive until spawning. For 2,000 eggs that is a 99. 9 percent casualty rate! So perhaps the students' fascination with the dead salmon is not a distraction after all. Certainly my focus on spawning underlines a distortion of the lifecycle diagram. The life-phases of salmon are of differing lengths: spawning, these few weeks of extreme group behavior, represents a mere one percent of the most short-lived salmon species' life. When Sockeye fry leave the nest, or "redd," most populations will spend one or two years inland, living in lakes, before heading to the ocean for another two to three years. Chum live three to five years, and their fry swim directly to the estuary, where they may spend time developing or continue to the ocean. For most salmon, the long, solitary, ocean-foraging phase of their lives is the least well-known.

The tidy lifecycle diagram also obscures accidental and intentional human intervention. Prior to the industrialization of salmon fishing, humans were among the predators sustained by stable populations. Over the past century, overfishing and inland development, including dams, mining, logging, agriculture, and urban expansion, have reduced the number of salmon in both marine and fresh water.

Some human interventions increase the survival rate of salmon. The spawning channel is one such example. Sexually mature adults spawn, and their eggs, alevins, and fry develop in an environment that, while still outdoors and under trees, is carefully curated. Hatcheries are a more intensive and more controversial intervention. Since the 1970s, the United States and Canada have invested heavily in hatcheries as the front line and chief avenue for salmon recovery. In major hatcheries, in the most extreme cases, all migrating salmon are removed from a stream, euthanized, and stripped of their gametes. Eggs are fertilized, disinfected, and incubated, and the resulting fry are fed and reared in protective tanks and then released—sometimes into the same stream, sometimes elsewhere. At the other end of the scale are less industrial hatcheries run by First Nations and other communities. The salmon Leona showed the students had passed through the Little Campbell River Hatchery. Run by the local fish and game club, all the salmon in the river, a modest 3,500 each year, are trapped and counted. Most are released to spawn, while a small number are removed for breeding stock. The hatchery supplies eggs for classrooms and hosts hundreds of school children for their first encounter with wild salmon.

In the wild, the egg-to-smolt survival rate can vary widely depending on year, species, and population, but it is a period of extremely high mortality. In hatcheries, nearly 75 percent of eggs become smolts. Each spring, nearly 300,000,000 hatchery-raised fry are released in British Columbia (globally five billion into the North Pacific) but the returns are disappointing. Hatcheries are subject to critique for a number of reasons. They are a technological fix for an ecological problem and increasing survivorship in one part of the lifecycle does not address the root causes of population decline. The initial focus of hatcheries was on increasing the overall number of salmon for commercial and sport fishing and repopulating streams where salmon were extirpated due to human activity. Sometimes there was even a nod to Indigenous traditional use. The result is that there are more salmon, but with reduced reproductive fitness and genetic diversity. Until recently, most hatchery salmon came from a small pool of eggs, with little thought given to the connection between broodstock and their river of origin. This creates a problem of "unnatural selection," where tank-fed fry outnumber and thus outcompete hardier wild fish, but then go on to experience greater mortality in the marine environment. Hatchery salmon are also incredibly expensive: a Washington state audit in 2002 calculated the average cost of a single adult hatchery salmon, factoring in facilities, staff, administration, and capital costs, ranges from $14 to a whopping $530 USD, with most averaging between $50 and $150. Despite these interventions, salmon populations continue to decline.

From the spawning channel, we drove to an open-walled shelter near the banks of the Fraser. Under the sweeping prow of a traditional river-going canoe, the students met Eddie Gardner, the elder who hosted the salmon ceremony in January. Eddie told the students about why salmon matter to him. Prior to contact with Europeans, the Coast Salish diet was 90 percent marine protein, a huge proportion of which was salmon. Eddie told the students that Salmon's constancy and generosity in feeding the forest, animals, and people is a moral example to the Sto:lo, the Indigenous people of the Fraser Valley.

A number of years ago I had the privilege of visiting a fish camp further up the Fraser canyon and witnessing dip-net fishing and wind drying. While the traditional fishing and food processing technologies were fascinating, I was most struck by each family's web of relationships and obligations that allowed this precious food resource to permeate a much broader community than just those with access to the river. No one caught fish for just one household.

Hearing Eddie speak about centuries of reciprocity between his people and the Salmon People, I remembered another Sto:lo salmon defender. I met Kwitsel Tatel on the winter solstice in 2017 at a spontaneous blockade on the route of the Trans Mountain Expansion Project, an economically and environmentally expensive pipeline that threatens salmon and humans. A rabbi chanted psalms, a deacon held a lighted candle, and a handful of us blocked trucks from entering the tank facility while Kwitsel drummed and sang in the snow.

In 2004, after nearly a decade and more than 200 court appearances, Kwitsel, or Patricia Kelly as she is also known, won compensation and an absolute discharge on charges of possessing salmon without a permit. Her argument was not based on the Western notion of rights, but, like Eddie and the families at the fish camp upriver, she was adamant that to harvest and distribute salmon was a spiritual obligation.

Eddie warned the students about the pipeline expansion and another a human-caused threat to wild Pacific Salmon: fish farms. Most farmed salmon in British Columbia are non-native Atlantic Salmon, grown in open-mesh pens in marine waters. At any one time there are approximately 80 active farms in British Columbia, each with up to three-quarters of a million fish in several net pens. The farms, 90 percent of which are Norwegian-owned, are distributed on the coast, along the routes of wild juvenile salmon heading to the ocean and adults migrating inland to spawn. The close quarters in these fish pens can be incubators for diseases like piscine reovirus, which damages the salmon's capacity for oxygen uptake. Seventy percent of farmed salmon carry this disease and may transmit it to wild salmon, reducing their endurance and impairing their ability to migrate for spawning. Sea lice from adult farmed salmon can infest migrating juvenile wild salmon, and escaped farmed salmon compete with the wild fish for scarce resources. Due to these risks, open-net farms have been banned on the Pacific coast of the United States, and Eddie, marine biologist Alexandra Morton, and others have worked tirelessly towards a similar ban here. Eddie begged the students to honour the salmon they had just met by refusing to eat farmed salmon.

Eddie pulled out his drum, and as he sang the salmon song an American Kestrel landed on a fence beside us, a tiny member of the falcon family with blue-grey wings, a rusty back and dark vertical facial bars on each side of its eyes. As the little hunter settled down and the drum beats rose up, I worried less about whether I had successfully shared what was important and trusted just a little that Eddie, and the river, and the salmon's own fierce drive for survival would teach the students what they needed to know.

* * *

A few days after the students headed back to Pennsylvania, I made a solo trip to Weaver Creek in the late afternoon. Free from the need to be a good host or a teacher, I tried simply to pay attention. The activity had shifted; the pace seemed grim rather than frenetic, with hundreds, not thousands, of salmon determinedly going about their business. And here and there among the rocks, I could see small white- and peach-coloured eggs.

Almost all the salmon in the channel were Sockeye. Their bright red and green colour had faded, and many showed exposed patches of yellowish-white decaying flesh. I spent a long time watching a single pair, hoping to catch them in the act and witness eggs being fertilized. It was challenging to identify individuals, but these two were distinctive. The male's battered nose had been split into two pale horn-like projections, and his back from head to dorsal fin had been scraped white. The female had a yellowish-green vertical marking between her first and second (pectoral and pelvic) fins on the left side. She also had two sea lice on her pectoral fin, indicating that she had been in fresh water for under a week. While these salmon travel fewer than 150 kilometres from the ocean, the Yukon River Chinook can migrate over 3,000 kilometres!

When salmon mate, the female selects a site with a gravel bottom, slight incline, and fast-moving water. She uses her tail to create a depression in the gravel, which she measures for depth with the curve of her body. The two salmon nudge and bump one another until the female lays some of her eggs; the male deposits sperm over them, then the female swims upstream and uses her tail to shovel gravel over the eggs. Sometimes a male who was not involved in the previous interactions will also deposit sperm over the eggs. Covering the eggs creates a new depression in which to lay more eggs. The female will move along to deposit eggs again, sometimes with another male. A female may have her eggs fertilized by three or more males. Males' reproductive success is more varied: some males fertilize many females' eggs and others few or none.

While California Sea Lions, Great Blue Herons, and Little Brown Bats invest a great deal of time and energy in a very few offspring, salmon don't do a lot of parenting. A female salmon will select and dig a redd and defend it and her eggs until she dies, but salmon's investment in their young is like that of the Looper Moths and Western Toads, who have many offspring in the hope that a few will survive.

When I first arrived, the female with the sea lice on her fin had staked out an area about the size of two single mattresses laid end to end. The male swam nearby and initially took the more active role, swimming above the female in the pattern called "cross-overs" and inserting his body between her and other males. The conventional wisdom holds that spawning salmon exhibit "intra-sex aggression," which means that females fight females for access to redds, and males fight males for access to females. While this female definitely made aggressive darts at other females, she appeared to be choosing her mate as well, swimming under him when he moved away and actively seeking out his presence. Although I watched for perhaps 30 minutes and the pair engaged in all the right behaviours—gaping, shoveling, shimmying—I never did see them spawn.

I followed the groomed spawning channel to the place where it splits off from the creek itself. Looking down, I could see perhaps 50 Chum resting in pools below as they made their way upstream. The dark midline stripe of the females was very obvious, and from above they seemed much larger than the Sockeye in the channel. Several made spectacular jumps of over a metre and a half, some clearing rocks and rapids, while others smashed their bodies hard against them. As I watched, the men in the salmon truck came around, chivvying visitors out of the park before closing time.

Reluctantly I headed back to the parking area, dawdling along the high bank of the stream. The sharp snap of a breaking branch drew my attention across the creek. A fat Black Bear had pulled a Chum from the water. It paused a moment, looking at me, and backed into the undergrowth. I wished the students had been there to see this completion of the circle from egg to salmon and predator to forest.

* * *

My final salmon trip of the year was in early November. On the way to a conference on new or alternative churches, I stopped at Goldstream Park on Vancouver Island, just north of Victoria. The river's English name comes from the mid-19th century gold rush, while the W̱SÁNEĆ name sʔǿləqʷtəł, refers to the people living downstream for whom it has been a traditional fishery for generations. I used to see salmon spawn at Goldstream as a child, visits that were most memorable for the smell of rotting fish and large numbers of gulls and Bald Eagles waiting to feast on them. As I arrived, the setting sun was making ribbons of pink on a blue sky under a quarter moon. I left my car just outside the park gates and walked toward the water in the gathering dark. The air smelled faintly fishy, and the trees were mostly silhouettes. The sound of rushing water was broken by bloops and splashes, like an energetic toddler in the bath.

Darkness made the water opaque, but I could see the spines of fish as they cut the surface. My friend Jeff, who snorkels in glacier-fed rivers for fun, talks about surface and depth from the unique perspective of one who knows both intimately. Standing waist-deep in the Capilano river, he once said to me, "This is how I talk with God. Most of us, most of the time, only see the surface of the river and we think it is flat, but when you are in the water a whole other dimension that was always there opens up." Toes to the water's edge, I contemplated the inky surface.

Unbothered by my presence, a pair of salmon swam close: they thrashed sinuously at my feet, splashing my pant leg; a few drops of water even touched my face in a kind of primal benediction. I felt humbled, or perhaps willingly diminished, by my proximity to such strength and urgency of purpose. I lingered until all I could see were dark shapes and the occasional glinting of light off of backs and fins. When I finally broke the connection and headed for my car, a uniformed ranger with a flashlight was making a final sweep of the parking lot. Just before I closed my car door, the metal gate clanged closed like an off-key church bell.

I returned early the next morning, and the colours were what I remembered—misty grey, green, pale pink, and yellowish decay. I cannot find an attribution for a quote that goes something like, "home is the place where the rocks look right." But this place for me is Vancouver Island. The shape of Arbutus twisting away from the water, asymetrical wind-ravaged Firs, and bare glacier-scraped rock exposed in long stretches. I like a place where you can see the land's bones. And the color of these salmon spawning feels right to me as well.

There were so many! Fish in the water, dead fish washed up against the irregular creek banks, and carcasses littering the ground. In the shadow of a bridge I could see fish in groups and in pairs and a lot of inter-male aggression. Males were darting at each other, chasing one another across the width of the stream, using their hooked jaws to grasp each other around the base of the tail.

The stream was flat, fairly fast-moving, and about as deep as the fish were high. In smooth water, I could see a few pale eggs between the rocks that ranged in size from walnut to coconut. From the bank, I tried to count every fish I could see without moving: 67. I changed position and counted again: 84. As with Weaver Creek, my eyes were drawn to individuals or pairs, but it was hard to get a sense of the big picture. How many salmon made up this gathering, and what do you call a gathering of salmon? The only mention of salmon in Dame Juliana's *Boke of Seynt Albans* is in a list of proper terms for dressing meat. Some lists of collective nouns call a group of trout a *hover*, which is appealing. The Old English word for multitudes gives us *shoals*, which is nice but not salmon-specific. The Halq'emeylum language, on the other hand, is too specific, with 147 identified words related to catching and processing fish—including Coho, Sockeye, and names for different sizes of each species, and names for the various phases of spawning. The name Chinook comes from a widespread Indigenous trade jargon from the Columbia River region. The name of the genus, *Oncorhynchus,* means lump-nosed, and refers to the hooked jaw, or *kype*, that develops in the male of some species prior to spawning. To further complicate matters, in English each of the five British Columbia salmon is known by several different common names, so a Chum is also a Dog Salmon and a Keta. A *run* is the term that I grew up hearing for salmon returning to their birthplace to spawn. It refers as much to the activity as the group, and while it isn't an entertaining term, nor is it centuries old, using it feels like an affirmation that, even though it has been mostly in the schoolroom and at the dinner table, I also have a relationship to the keystone species of the watershed where I live.

The natural stream and the surrounding forest were complex and varied compared to the uniform salmon channel. The trees along the bank were wrapped in thick green moss. Ferns grew on trunks and branches high above my head. The forest was alive with birds, American Dippers bending and feeding, zigzagging from bank to bank; a Belted Kingfisher chattered as it flew downstream; and overhead I could hear the fluting calls of two Bald Eagles. A heron landed with a grunting squawk and began slowly stalking along the edge of the water. I followed it for a good 15 minutes, hoping to witness what I have only seen on video: a Great Blue Heron swallowing a whole salmon. Eventually it flew off, empty beak and empty gullet. The real bird show, however, was the gulls. Glaucous-Winged

Gulls, big birds with pink feet, white heads, and grey wings, paddled inches from the unbothered fish, mewing loudly. I assumed that the carcasses on the banks were what drew the gulls until I saw one wade into the stream, stamp furiously, and dip its head under water. They were disturbing the rocks and feeding on the protein-rich salmon eggs, even as the fish were laying them.

Globally, marine life is dwindling, and the oceans are in trouble. For much of my lifetime, and accelerating in recent years, headlines about Pacific Salmon stocks, once thought to be inexhaustible, have featured words like "disastrous," "dire," "hard-hit," and "collapse." We no longer see "June hogs" and "Fraser hogs"—massive Chinook weighing more than 45 kilograms. Much of the data regarding salmon is difficult to interpret, because populations fluctuate greatly from year to year and the focus has been on counting the fish caught, not the number remaining in the ocean. Nevertheless, it is estimated that despite massive restoration efforts, over the past century Fraser River salmon have been reduced to between one-half and one-eighth of their numbers, due mostly to overfishing and habitat loss. Many small populations have ceased to exist, and the remaining salmon are smaller than those of previous generations, negatively impacting the many species that depend on them.

Scientists at Canada's first "State of the Salmon" meeting in 2018 concluded that Canadian Pacific Salmon and their ecosystems were already responding to climate change. Ocean warming trends and marine heat waves impact food webs. Inland air and water temperatures are increasing and precipitation patterns are changing. Less snow, earlier melting, more frequent summer droughts and heat waves are altering freshwater habitats. Salmon are affected throughout their lives, in every habitat they move through, at every stage of their life-cycle.

At the peak of industrialization, only half a century after John Sullivan Deas opened the first, there were eighty canneries in British Columbia, producing tens of thousands of cases of salmon for export and domestic consumption. Now there is one. It is both ironic and hopeful that the last operating cannery in the province is owned by a partnership of Nuu-chah-nulth nations.

In the quote that opens this chapter, the governor of Acadia makes a haunting comparison between the Passenger Pigeon and the Atlantic Salmon as he complains of being kept awake at night by the noise of spawning. On the Pacific coast, there are accounts from both settlers and Indigenous people that describe salmon so numerous that "you could cross the river on their backs." At Weaver Creek, it was the numbers of salmon that made me catch my breath. Even at the manicured spawning channel, seeing thousands of salmon thick in the water was like a glimpse into the past, when creeks and rivers teemed. Visiting Goldstream, I was more aware of the integration of the salmon into their environment and the way that their intense physical urgency was part of a greater pattern that includes herons, eagles, gulls, and trees. Their return to place was echoed in my own return to the grey and green landscape that I had loved in my childhood. Standing on the riverbank, I watched an egg spin away in the current. A single vertebra at my feet was the same size and colour. I bent to pick it up and I prayed that the students, my own children, but especially Eddie's grandchildren, would be able to carry on relationships of respect and reciprocity with the Salmon's children.

SOURCES AND RESOURCES

Ebb & Flow: Turning Points in West Coast Fishing History

Gulf of Georgia Cannery Society and Port Edward Historical Society, 2018
A 25-minute film that documents key historical, sociological and technological milestones in British Columbia's fishing industry. With material
on the diverse cultural and socioeconomic groups highlighting Indigenous
fisheries and the influence of the Japanese community. It is screened daily
at the Gulf of Georgia Cannery.

Gulf of Georgia Cannery

12138 Fourth Avenue, Richmond, BC, Canada
Established in 1894 and once the largest producer of canned salmon in
Canada, the cannery is now an interactive museum on the West Coast
fishing industry that gives particular attention to race, class, gender, and
the environment.

"Historical Perspectives on Inland Fisheries Management"

By Christine M. Moffitt, Gary Whelan, and Randy Jackson
American Fisheries Society, 2010
In *Inland Fisheries Management in North America* 3rd Edition
This dry but comprehensive opening chapter in a textbook on fisheries
management is the source of the 1672 quote from the Acadian governor
Denys who was kept awake by spawning salmon.

"The Last BC Cannery Standing—and Why It Matters"

By Frances Backhouse
The Tyee, August 22, 2018
In a news magazine whose namesake is a giant salmon, this journalistic
history of the salmon canning industry in British Columbia focuses on the
significance of the Nuu-chah-nulth-owned St. Jean's cannery.

"Malnourished Millennial Killer Whales Grew Up Smaller"

By Jaspreet Sahib
Hakai Magazine, January 10, 2020
A short, readable article on how plummeting Chinook stock have impacted juvenile resident Orca, written for an online journal of coastal science.

Not On My Watch: How a Renegade Whale Biologist Took on Governments and Industry to Save Wild Salmon

By Alexandra Morton
Random House Canada, 2021
Whale researcher Alexandra Morton describes how she shifted her focus from resident Orcas to documenting the impacts of infectious diseases and parasites from farmed Atlantic Salmon on wild Pacific Salmon. Her account includes collaboration between scientists, fishing communities, and First Nations.

"Pacific Salmon Abundance Trends in the Fraser River Watershed Compared with Other British Columbia Systems"

By T. G. Northcote and D. Y. Atagi
Springer Science + Business Media, 1997
In *Pacific Salmon and their Ecosystems: Status and Future Options*
A scholarly article in an academic anthology. The writing is clear and accessible and the title accurately describes the content.

A Salmon for Simon

By Betty Waterton, illustrated by Ann Blades
Groundwood Books/House of Anansi, 1978
This lovely picture book has been through multiple reprints. It tells the story of the relationship between a coastal First Nation boy and a salmon.

Speaking for the Salmon

By Jonathan Moore, Arne Mooers, and Patricia Gallaugher
Simon Fraser University, 2017
A short report from a two-day think tank of salmon experts from the scientific community, First Nations, non-governmental organizations, and government. The report is organized into nine findings and subsequent recommendations for a science-based policy for wild Pacific Salmon restoration.

State of the Canadian Pacific Salmon: Responses to Changing Climate and Habitats

By S.C.H. Grant, B.L. MacDonald, and M.L. Winston
Fisheries and Oceans Canada, 2019
A detailed Department of Fisheries and Oceans report on the way Pacific Salmon are imperilled by climate change and loss of biodiversity. It recommends more research, decreased greenhouse gas emissions, and "adaptation" in salmon enhancement practices.

"Struggling Downstream"

By Mark Hume
Globe and Mail, September 16, 2016
A popular article outlining scientists' questions about the population numbers, expense, and genetic impacts of British Columbia's fish hatcheries on wild Pacific Salmon populations.

Urban Salmon: A Photographic Journey into the Metro Vancouver Watershed

Written and photographed by Fernando Lessa
Fernando Lessa Photography & Storytelling, 2019
This beautiful collection of vibrant underwater colour photographs of salmon, was taken in the network of small streams around the city of Vancouver. Photos are captioned with detailed information about the lives and ecosystems of urban salmon.

WILDLIFE CONGREGATIONS

A Gaggle of Geese

8

Goosey, goosey gander where shall I wander?
Upstairs and downstairs and in my lady's chamber.
There I met an old man who wouldn't say his prayers
So I took him by the left leg and threw him down the stairs.

English Nursery Rhyme, 18th century

My first sighting of Snow Geese this year was at the Reifel Migratory Bird Sanctuary on Westham Island, a small sediment island of mostly farms in the Fraser River delta. It was during the Villanova University students' visit, and the chief attraction for the students was that human-habituated Black-Capped Chickadees, Red-Winged Blackbirds, and at least one bold Red-Breasted Nuthatch would feed from our hands. The trip was more raucous and boisterous than the kind of careful stepping and silent observation I am used to when I take a camera or binoculars out to see birds: the appearance of a low-flying Bald Eagle caused the students to burst into patriotic song.

As we walked on the West Dike Trail close to the water, Snow Geese were visible in the tidal shallows perhaps half a kilometre away, a shimmering, whitish-grey flock of hundreds, emitting high mewing cries. As the eagle passed over them, the entire flock rose to form a low cloud, uttering sharp alarm calls more raucous than the students and easily audible at our distance. Then, as quickly as they rose, the birds settled again.

A small, whitish goose with dark wing-tips, the Snow Goose is shaped more like a domestic duck than the aggressive, snakey-necked Canada Geese that monopolize city parks, or the tough-as-nails barnyard geese that used to guard my father's house. Family lore says that the dog brought the first one home, and my father was summoned by a cacophony of honking, hissing, and growling to find the spaniel pulling a gander up the lawn a step at a time with one wing in its soft mouth while the enraged bird beat the dog about the head with its free wing. The bird stayed, and from time to time neighbours would leave unwanted geese on the property until there was a small flock. (Domestic geese can live for more than twenty years.) Most geese form long-term pair-bonds, and after his mate died the original gander paired for over a year with a horse that was boarded on the property; they could often be seen following one another around the pasture.

Snow Geese were part of this book when it consisted of nothing more than a list of animal gatherings and their collective names. A *gaggle* of geese, which comes from the Middle English word for cackle, is perhaps the best known of Dame Juliana's terms of venery, and certainly it is one of the few in common usage. Gaggle refers to geese on the ground, as do the terms *flock* and the lesser known *plump*. Since the early 15th century, gaggle has also been used to describe a group of gossiping humans. Geese in the air are referred to as a *wedge* if they fly in a triangular pattern or a *skein* if they form long strings.

I knew that Snow Geese gathered in the Lower Mainland each winter, but they had always been peripheral to me, seen in fields from car windows. I did not know very much about them, so after seeing the flock at Reifel Sanctuary I did some research online. I learned that there are two subspecies of Snow Geese. The birds that gather on the West Coast are Lesser Snow Geese, a small to medium-size goose weighing about 2.5 kilograms, or as much as a brick. They live for 10 to 20 years, breeding in the High Arctic and migrating south in the winter to food-rich estuaries. The slightly larger Greater Snow Goose is similar in appearance and ecology, breeding in Nunavut along the coastal areas, High Arctic islands as well as Hudson Bay. They migrate through the Atlantic, Mississippi, and Central Flyways to the Eastern Seaboard and Gulf Coast of North America. Unlike the majority of wild birds, Snow Geese have increased in range and number in recent years. The large mid-continent population, which migrates through the central agricultural belt of North America to Texas and the Gulf Coast, has increased so much in the past four decades that it is causing great damage to the fragile tundra in its central Arctic breeding ground.

In early November I went by myself to Boundary Bay, a body of water bisected by the Canada-US border where Snow Geese gather in large numbers. When I arrived at the beach park, the tide was out. I saw rolling grassy fields, an expanse of exposed shore, distant water, and the occasional gull but no geese. I headed northeast, following the curve of the bay along a path marked Raptor Trail. The raptors did not disappoint; within ten minutes I had seen eight Northern Harriers coasting low and diving feet-first into the grass, hunting rodents. A long-tailed, broad-winged hunter also called a Marsh Hawk, the Harriers' distinctive white rumps made them easy to spot. The trail curved away from the water's edge into scrubby grassland. As I walked, perhaps a kilometre and a half to the east, a clamoring cloud of white specks rose up briefly and disappeared—the geese! I craned my neck, searching for landmarks. They were on the other side of the road that brought me to the park, but a quick consultation with Google maps showed no direct route from park to geese. Undeterred, I headed for the parking lot.

As I approached the car park and the water was visible again, I could see far out by the receding tide, across a shiny, wet expanse of silt, the shifting shape of hundreds of feeding shore birds—another group that I planned to visit this year. Turning my back on the inaccessible geese, I strode along the boardwalk towards the sand, my eyes fixed on the shore birds, until I heard another great chorus of harsh cries behind me. Snow Geese have a reputation as the loudest of geese, and their calls are audible from more two kilometres. I turned to see a flock of at least 1,000 rise up, remaining visible in the air for several minutes. I hesitated, caught between the shorebirds, across untraversable mud flats, and the cloud of Snow Geese, rising and falling at some inland place I couldn't identify and probably couldn't reach by road.

The cloud of geese appeared again, and I stomped to my car. After impolitely dislodging two cyclists who, from all the vast and almost completely unoccupied parking lot, had chosen the square metre behind my rear bumper to stop and discuss electoral ridings, I set off driving. As usual I was looking too much at the sky and too little at the road, only drawing my eyes back down to correct my drift. My plan was, essentially, to find the geese by triangulation, driving as close to them as the roads would allow.

When I located them, the Snow Geese were far out in a farmer's field amid a crop that seemed to consist of rows of tiny sticks. The field was bordered on one side by a long, and—as was adamantly sign-posted in red—PRIVATE driveway. The other edge of the field was marked by a tiny cul-de-sac and some heavy equipment indicating that some sort of development was underway. Neither of these seemed to say, "Welcome nature enthusiasts."

I decided to brazen it out and walk through the construction site. Quite unnecessarily, I told the curious and then bewildered guy loading small diggers onto a flatbed, that I was part of a conservation project.

Work on the proto-road had thrown up a clay berm that shielded me from the sight of the geese as I clambered slowly across the uneven ground towards them. Over the wall of earth I could hear their calls, a high repeated mew, less strident than their call in air. Occasionally a small group of 20 to 30 would rise up into view and resettle. The road ended in a flat area crisscrossed with tractor tracks, and I gained about a kilogram in clay on each of my boots as I crossed it. The field was filled with thousands of geese, and a second water-filled field beyond held a similar number.

They were a moving mass of white and grey. Their black primary feathers, striking in flight, were almost invisible on the ground. When I finally rounded the corner, the entire flock was visible, stretching in both directions for perhaps a kilometre. They formed a rough teardrop shape only 15 or 20 geese wide near me and much wider towards the flooded field. The geese closest to me were six or seven metres away, close enough to see their eyes and to make out some detail, but they were such a mass, their identity so essentially corporate, that I couldn't focus on a single individual; my eyes kept sliding over them.

The geese seemed to respect each other's space, keeping an even distance between them as they moved back and forth. Most were digging in the ground, feeding. Snow Geese bills are equipped with serrated cutting edges on both upper and lower surfaces for severing roots; this darker line that makes them look like they are smiling is aptly named a "grinning patch." Those who already find geese threatening will be horrified to know that this Joker's grimace also hides a sharp, serrated tongue.

For tens of thousands of years, Snow Geese fed on the energy-rich rhizomes of wintering marsh plants, but with the conversion of marshland to agricultural and residential use in the Fraser Delta and elsewhere in their habitat, the geese have moved their foraging inland and diversified their diet. Since the 1980s, the Snow Goose population in this area has nearly doubled, and their marshland diet is supplemented with the roots of grass from sports fields and parks, and field waste from farm crops. The bills and feet of thousands of geese can very quickly churn a field into a lake of standing water, mud, and shit. Speaking of the proverbial goose shit, food moves rapidly through a Snow Goose's digestive tract, generating six to 15 droppings per hour. Although they eat more in the tundra, their defecation rate is highest when grubbing for high-fibre rhizomes. To protect economically and ecologically sensitive areas from destruction, the cities of Delta and Richmond have had some success partnering with farmers to plant decoy crops of cereal grasses like barley and oats to attract hungry Snow Geese.

Lesser Snow Geese nest in the Arctic, most of them on islands and coastal areas of Alaska and Northern Canada. The geese that winter in the Lower Mainland, however, breed on Wrangel Island in Siberia and migrate across the Bering Strait to Alaska then south along the west coast of the continent, some travelling as far as California. During migration they fly night and day and can reach speeds of up to 80 kilometres per hour.

Wrangel Island comprises about 7,000 square kilometres; in local terms it is about one-fifth the size of Vancouver Island, or a little larger than Graham Island, the largest of the Haida Gwaii archipelago. It is a protected nature sanctuary and a United Nations World Heritage Site, with the highest level of biodiversity in the High Arctic. This includes the world's greatest density of Polar Bear dens, largest population of Pacific Walrus, and more species of plants than any other Arctic island in the world. It is visited by more than 100 species of migratory birds and is the last place on earth where Woolly Mammoths survived! The Wrangel Island Snow Geese have made a tremendous comeback since the 1970s but are considered a critical subgroup because they are the only Snow Geese that breed on the Asian continent. Researchers on the island distinguish our Fraser-Skagit sub-population from the California-wintering birds by the rust-coloured stains on their faces caused by the iron-rich Fraser delta soil. In late fall, upwards of 80,000 arrive at the mouth of the Fraser; approximately half will continue farther south to the Skagit Delta in Washington State, and the rest remain here for the winter.

In the field I sat myself down on a cold lump of clay that made an acceptable stool. Sheltered from wind by the wall of raised earth behind me, with the sun warm on my face and bright on the yellow farmhouse across the field, it was as pleasant a November day as I could have hoped for.

The geese continued to call and feed, and small groups of 10 or so would rise and resettle, responding to no provocation that I could detect. I secretly hoped a Bald Eagle would come by and cause the flock to take flight, as they had done at Reifel Sanctuary. The geese did not seem afraid of me, but they kept their distance. Often the grey-coloured juveniles were closest to me; I wondered if perhaps they were less wary, or if their low status pushed them to the edge of the flock. But after learning more about their growing population, I suspect that juveniles might simply have outnumbered the adults.

The number of Snow Geese has been rising since the 1970s; it is estimated that there are five million Lesser Snow Geese in North America, an increase of 300 percent since the mid-1970s, with an additional one million Greater Snow Geese. The Fraser-Skagit population has increased from between 30,000 and 50,000 in the 1980s to a high of over 100,000 in 2017. This increase is due to restrictions on hunting and the birds' easy dietary transition from wild marsh grass to agricultural crops. Increasing Arctic temperatures mean less snow, which, despite their name, is actually an advantage for Snow Geese. With more snow-free days in the nutrient-rich north, young geese make their first migration larger and stronger than their predecessors. In the eastern Arctic, the increased numbers of geese are actually damaging the food production capacity of their nesting and staging grounds, not just for themselves but for other species as well. There is concern that western populations may also become unsustainable. The conservation phenomenon of "overabundant" populations is relatively new, and while there are some signs that the populations will be limited naturally as the carrying capacity of their habitat is reached, possible interventions like culls or changes in hunting limits would involve international conversations between Canada, the United States, and Russia.

Unlike most waterfowl, Lesser Snow Geese nest in large colonies with densities up to 5,000 pair per square kilometre, or, in more relatable terms, 10 nests in an area the size of single bed mattress. They arrive in late spring and begin mating, often in the water. Lesser Snow Geese form lifelong pair bonds, but they are not sexually monogamous; females will mate with nearby males when their partners are absent from the nest, and males will seek out other females once their own mates have finished laying eggs. These "extra-pair couplings," as they are called, give males the opportunity to increase the number of their offspring, and females the opportunity to diversify the fitness of theirs, while the benefits of pair bonding include shared parenting duties and protection of offspring.

If by mid-June the Arctic ground is still covered in snow, females can reabsorb their unlaid eggs and forgo nesting for that year. The Snow Goose nest is a depression in gravel or moss, and a clutch consists of two to six eggs. Females incubate the eggs for about 23 days, rarely leaving the nest, and can lose up to one-third of their body weight during this time. Males defend the nest from predators like Arctic Foxes and sea birds, and from other geese seeking a nest. Sometimes an invading female will lay an egg nearby as part of a takeover attempt. The goose on the nest will incorporate the egg into her clutch rather than risk it attracting predators, further increasing the complexity of goose-family genetics. Unlike Northwestern Crows and Great Blue Herons, whose altricial hatchlings are helpless and must be fed, geese have precocial (same root word as precocious) babies. Within hours of hatching, goslings are able to walk, swim, and forage; parental care consists mainly of defense from predators. When all the eggs have hatched, the entire family leaves the nest and the remainder of the summer is dedicated to walking and eating grass and sedges so that adults and young are large and strong enough to migrate. They need all the calories they can get. Young geese increase their weight 12-fold in less than four weeks, and the adults undergo an energetically costly moult. A family of geese can travel five kilometres in a day, eating for 12 hours. In contrast, wintering geese in Richmond spend less than half that time feeding.

Despite my hopes, the sky and the surrounding trees remained steadfastly eagle-free. From time to time a Northern Harrier would buzz the edge of the flock, causing groups of about 50 geese to fly up, calling in alarm, but they resettled quickly. My pre-trip online goose tutorial indicated that while most Snow Geese are white with dark wingtips, some exhibit a blue or "dark morph," with a slate-grey body and white head. I scanned the flock, hoping to catch sight of one, but all I saw was white and pale grey. More thorough research later revealed that the blue morph is very rare in the Fraser-Skagit population, but I found it revealing that on this quest to experience the collective, I found myself searching for the unique individual, the stand-out in the crowd. I wondered about my inability to appreciate and give full attention to the flock itself. Was it evidence of being steeped in a Western culture that venerates the individual and neglects the collective, or a reflection of my own fear of conformity?

I watched the geese for perhaps an hour, until the cold seeping up from my clay seat made my hips stiff. Just as I stood up, ready to leave, the Bald Eagle I had been waiting for materialized and flew low over the flock. Hundreds of birds started up in alarm. Like some avian Red Sea before Moses and Miriam, the cloud of perhaps 1,000 split in two, some flying towards the road, the others joining the flock in the flooded field to the west.

I have heard a flock of Snow Geese taking flight being described as "like being inside a shaken snow globe." That was not my experience. A snow globe is a small, enclosed population flying about at random. The geese vastly outnumbered the flakes in a snow globe, and there was a very clear pattern to their movement. When they took flight, each individual shot up four or five metres into the air, then paused to take stock of the birds nearby. They all oriented to one another and began to form lines and undulating strings heading in a single direction. The name *skein* suddenly made sense to me, and I was struck by the contrast to the ragged patterns crows make when they fly.

This habit of exploding straight up into the air makes Snow Geese especially dangerous around airplanes. The Vancouver International Airport, located on another island in the Fraser delta, employs a wildlife management team that uses lasers, pyrotechnics, noise-cannons, dogs, and trained raptors to keep geese and other birds away from the airfield.

They have also partnered with the federal government and local farmers to plant winter cover crops to lure geese and other waterfowl away from the airport to neighbouring municipalities.

The skeins settled and I began to walk along the inside of the clay berm, hoping to make a shorter way back to my vehicle while still in proximity to the geese. The birds were restless and moved away from me, their necks swiveling like a field of living periscopes.

Suddenly something changed, and a ripple of awareness seemed to move through the group—perhaps they were still restless from the eagle; more likely I had come too close. The entire flock took wing. What must certainly have been 10,000 birds were the air over my head. As they flew, their cries became coordinated, and the sound changed from a shrill kind of mewing to an almost mechanical pulsing, like hammers smashing against metal in waves, or industrial machine parts scraping against each other. It was such an auditory assault that I thought it might push me to the ground.

At some point, things changed visually as well. At first, any individual that I fixed my eyes on was a clear and distinct self, but as they moved up and away, the repeated line of bill, wing, and eye turned into video static or dirty grey scribbles. They didn't so much merge with one another as they became a collective entity, not 10,000 geese but something else. This, like the rolling motion of California Sea Lion tonnage undulating off the rocks, was the collective. This was what I was seeking as I pursued these aggregations of creatures, to be obliterated just a little by the vastness of something else.

How would my sense of self—my importance, my capacity—be different if I were regularly deafened by the rising and falling of thousands? If I shared space with them? Attended to them seasonally? Relied on them for food?

And then the moment passed. As the geese moved away, they resolved again into distinguishable individual forms and voices. The entire flock assembled in the flooded field to the east. And I took my clay-heavy boots home.

SOURCES AND RESOURCES

Chief Goose

By Mike Bowden, illustrated by Kelsey Jules
Strong Nations Publishing, 2020
Chief Goose Kúkwpi7 K'wsucw uses traditional practice, listening, and leadership to bring his people, the Canada Geese, to a safe place for the winter. A contemporary Secwepemc picture book about migration and Indigenous worldviews, for middle-school aged readers.

Delta Farmland and Wildlife Trust

An innovative nonprofit that partners with local farmers to preserve both farmland and wildlife habitat on the lower Fraser River delta through cooperative land stewardship including soil restoration, winter crops for geese, and hedgerows for songbirds. Their website includes information about their programs and local wildlife.
deltafarmland.ca

Ducks Unlimited

An 80-year-old organization started by hunters to preserve wetlands and associated waterfowl habitat through partnerships with various stakeholders. Their website contains media and resources for conservation and education.
ducks.ca

George C. Reifel Migratory Bird Sanctuary

5191 Robertson Road, Delta, BC, Canada
Nearly 300 walkable hectares of managed wetlands, marshes, and dykes in the Fraser River Estuary. Almost 300 species of birds have been recorded in the sanctuary, with greatest diversity in numbers from spring to fall, when millions feed and rest during their coastal migrations. A fantastic destination for a day trip for students, families, and veteran birders.
reifelbirdsanctuary.com

"Natural System of Wrangel Island Reserve"

Clear and detailed information on Wrangel Island, a United Nations World Heritage Site that is host to incredible Arctic biodiversity.
whc.unesco.org/en/list/1023/

North American Ducks, Geese and Swans Identification Guide

By Frank S. Todd
Hancock House, 2018
This detailed photographic field guide includes range maps, illustrations and descriptions. It is the posthumously published work of a noted wildlife photographer and conservationist.

Pacific Flyway: Waterbird Migration from the Arctic to Tierra del Fuego

By Audrey DeLella Benedict, Geoffrey A. Hammerson, and Robert W. Butler
Sasquatch Books, 2020
A beautiful large-format collection of photographs conveying both the beauty and the science of waterbird migration.

The Raptors

1877 Herd Road, Duncan, BC, Canada
Also called Pacific Northwest Raptors this conservation, education and wildlife management organization uses applied falconry to keep problem species off landfills and airports. They have a visitor centre in Duncan and are enthusiastic promoters of the ecological role and importance of raptors around British Columbia.
pnwraptors.com

Snow Geese in the Lower Mainland of British Columbia

Environment and Climate Change Canada, 2016
A clear and user-friendly document to inform local residents and about the biology, habitat, and management of the region's tens of thousands of annual visitors.

A Convocation
of Eagles
9

During the early years of his banding, Mr. Broley used to find 125 active nests a year on the stretch of coast he had chosen for his work. The number of young banded each year was about 150. In 1947 the production of young birds began to decline. Some nests contained no eggs; others contained eggs that failed to hatch. Between 1952 and 1957, about 80 per cent of the nests failed to produce young. In the last year of this period only 43 nests were occupied. Seven of them produced young (8 eaglets); 23 contained eggs that failed to hatch; 13 were used merely as feeding stations by adult eagles and contained no eggs. In 1958 Mr. Broley ranged over 100 miles of coast before banding one eaglet.

Rachel Carson, 1962

A few years ago, my good friend Mary, who is also my daughter Harriet's godmother, travelled to Alaska from her home in Washington State, to visit the largest gathering-place of Bald Eagles in the world. She described walks where she saw dozens of eagles, sometimes ten or more in a single tree.

I didn't have the heart to tell her that the town of Brackendale, one hour north of Vancouver and only four hours north of where she lives, and Harrison Mills, on the Fraser, also claim to be the winter roost of the greatest number of Bald Eagles in the world. Even closer to her home, Bald Eagles gather in large numbers along the Skagit River, near the border between the United States and Canada. Each of these locations hosts an abundant salmon run.

The Bald Eagle is one of the best-known birds in North America; its species name *Haliaeetus leucocephalus,* which means "sea eagle, white head," succinctly describes both its habitat and appearance. With a striking white head and tail, dark brown body and wings, yellow talons and large hooked bill, this large raptor can be seen along coasts and waterways throughout North America. The Bald Eagle has a wingspan of about two metres, but, surprisingly, even the largest is outweighed by a good-sized housecat. Immature birds have darker heads and tails, and their brown wings and bodies are mottled with white. Young birds acquire adult plumage at about five years.

Fifty years ago, Bald Eagles were rare in North America. They had been trapped, poisoned as pests, and shot by fishers, farmers, and trophy hunters. Up until 1953, the state of Alaska offered a bounty on Bald Eagles and over 111,000 pairs of Bald Eagle feet were redeemed for payment. They suffered reproductive failure due to the use of DDT, an insecticide that washed into water systems and became concentrated as it moved up the aquatic food chain, causing egg fragility and beak deformities. In 1962, biologist Rachel Carson's book *Silent Spring* exposed the harms of indiscriminate pesticide use and ushered in an era of conservation in North America. While the massive loss of flying insect species has seen a corresponding drop in the small birds that feed on them, the banning of

DDT and protective legislation in the United States, Canada, and Mexico have enabled a tremendous resurgence in Bald Eagle numbers during my lifetime. The global breeding population is estimated at around 250,000.

A worthwhile aside: some inadvertent truths about the values of conservation and population biologists, and perhaps the rest of us, are revealed in the concept of "breeding population." When I, and I suspect many people, hear "breeding population," I mentally erase the word *breeding*, or if I think about it at all, I imagine that the term generally affirms the fact that the population as a whole is fertile. Breeding population actually refers to the number of sexually mature individuals within a group, presumed to be engaging in reproductive activity. In species like eagles and geese that form seasonal or long-term pair bonds, population is often expressed in terms of "breeding pairs." If we take the example of crows in my courtyard, the pair tending the nest, their three nestlings, two nest helpers—probably siblings from recent years—and a lone crow, eight in total, would have a breeding population of two individuals, or one breeding pair.

Like Northwestern Crows, Bald Eagles have adapted successfully to the urban environment. The number of active nests has increased from three in the city of Vancouver in 1960s to more than 500 across the Fraser Valley today. This increase has been amplified for me because, as the population has increased, my awareness and interest has also grown. Living in the heart of the city I see eagles often: perched on a construction site crane down the street, in the waterside park behind our housing co-op. Often a mob of yelling crows will draw my eyes to the bulky form of an eagle in a tree. In Victoria, neighbours of my aunt and uncle in tony Oak Bay had a nesting pair in a cedar tree in their back yard and would complain of the gull wings and fish heads dropped on their lawn.

Bald Eagles are opportunistic feeders, with fish making up much of their diet. When food is abundant, an individual can store up to two kilograms of meat, about four steaks' worth, in an extension of its esophagus called the crop. Fabulously, although not quite as dramatically as owls, who do not have a crop and cannot digest bone, eagles can accumulate indigestible bits, mostly feathers and fur, in the gizzard, the muscular part of the stomach where food is ground up. They will expel this, and by *expel* I mean vomit, later as a compact, mucus-covered "casting." Eagles can gorge, eating a large amount of food and digesting it over several days, and they can fast, going days and sometimes weeks without eating. As the increase in the North American Bald Eagle population has coincided with declining salmon population, Great Blue Herons, mostly chicks, are more often on the menu. Eagles also eat waterfowl and other birds, reptiles, and small mammals; there are even documented accounts of Bald Eagles successfully killing animals as large as fawns.

Eagles are often thought of as regal and powerful hunters, and Dame Juliana's treatise on falconry says that an emperor may hunt with an eagle, a king with a Gyrfalcon, a prince with a Peregrine, and so on in descending rank, until, almost at the bottom of the list, the Sparrowhawk is deemed the appropriate hunting bird for a priest. The the American Kestrel, the tiny falcon that joined Eddie Gardner as he sang to the students is sometimes called a Sparrowhawk, but the European Sparrowhawk is an accipiter, making our Sharp-shinned Hawk a more accurate North American counterpart. Both birds are smaller than a crow and hunt songbirds, rodents, and grasshoppers, so it is probably a good thing this priest is a vegetarian.

Any emperors hunting with Bald Eagles might find themselves disappointed as well. Bald Eagles frequently scavenge carrion, raid nests, and dine at the local landfill. They will also drive other hunters, or scavengers, away from a meal. Referring to this behavior, Benjamin Franklin famously regretted the Bald Eagle's choice as the national symbol of the United States, saying, "He is a bird of bad moral character; he does not get his living honestly."

* * *

In March, 10 days before my first visit to the heronry, I was fortunate to witness an amazing example of Bald Eagle feeding versatility. Hunting is energetically costly and not always successful; in terms of the ratio of calories spent for calories gained, scavenging and bullying are much more efficient. I was visiting Reifel Migratory Bird Sanctuary and, alerted by the noisy departure of a mixed group of waterfowl, I turned to see an immature Bald Eagle in the open water of the marsh, doing an ungainly breaststroke, drawing its wings through the water and swimming towards a partially submerged stump. It hauled itself up, pulling with it a Pintail Duck, and began to tear feathers from its breast. Over the next thirty minutes, in a series of interactions that involved six eagles, three trees, an underwater hiding place, two eagle pairs working in tandem, and the feeding hierarchy within the pair, the Pintail changed hands, or talons, four separate times. At one point, after confirming that its catch had indeed been stolen, the original bird hopped up and down on the stump in apparent outrage and frustration.

* * *

Eagles are scavengers as well as hunters, and a city provides a wealth of available protein in the form of road-kill and landfill waste. A few years ago, large numbers of Bald Eagles were attracted to a composting centre in Delta, and I went out to see. With a very poor camera, I took a shot where I can count 30 individuals perched on the ground and the big wheels supporting irrigation lines, and another dozen in the air. From the narrow public road, lined with the cars of eager birders, I stumbled onto private property where a cluster of photographers was gathered, looking up at an eagle on a rooftop eating a European Starling. A few seconds, or maybe 15 minutes, later, my reverie was interrupted by the homeowner honking her horn at the hunched forms behind long lenses blocking her driveway. Most of the other photographers were oblivious, but I scuttled out of the way, shrugging helplessly, as the woman glared and gestured. All she wanted was to get into her garage, but majesty and life and death were perched and bloody on her rooftop. I think her frustration and indifference are typical of all of us. We miss the Divine when it shows up because it is inconvenient, and messy, and we just need to get into the damned garage.

* * *

Learning that large numbers of Bald Eagles winter alongside the lower Fraser, I began to keep my eyes open for them. On a visit to Reifel Sanctuary, I was driving along River Road in Delta, which runs along the south arm of the Fraser. Out in the marshland, I could see several trees or clumps of trees, with eight or 10 or more eagles in each. The size of Bald Eagles and the fact that, as visual hunters, they tend to like a high perch, makes them easy to spot. I parked in a pull-out and followed a trail towards one of the eagle trees. The elevated path ran alongside a channel that seemed to be a local flyway. As I walked along, two or three eagles in succession drifted above the channel at tree-top height, then veered off into the marsh.

As the trees on the channel side of the path thinned out and disappeared, I spied an eagle approaching at a much lower altitude. Its flight-path seemed to include the treeless portion of the trail where I was walking. Most of the time when I see eagles they are high in a tree or soaring overhead. They are so big that, even at a distance, it is possible to make out a lot of detail—eyes, yellow talons, hooked bill—particularly with binoculars or a camera. But until I stood on that path with a Bald Eagle soaring towards me, I did not realize how truly enormous they are.

As with most raptors, female Bald Eagles are larger than males. While no one is certain why this is, there are several hypotheses to explain this kind of sexual dimorphism. For the most part, raptors are well-armed and aggressive species. Females may have selected for smaller males over time, by choosing smaller mates who are less physically dangerous to them. Females, who do the majority of brooding and feeding, may simply require the energetic reserves of a larger body for the work of parenting. Raptors who must hunt near their nest while feeding nestlings may have differentiated in size as specialization for different-sized prey, in order to reduce competition between mates.

As the eagle approached, I first felt a kind of glorious anticipation, chanting under my breath, "Yes, c'mon, fly right by here, you beautiful thing. That's right, come this way, here, right here." And then, as the giant wings moved closer, I experienced a more crudely expressed awe—"Holy shit!"—and the abject certainty and exhilarated terror that I would be struck off the path. A two-metre wingspan in the air or in a treetop is a different thing altogether from a two-metre wingspan speeding at you along a three-metre-wide trail.

Maybe the eagle altered its course, or maybe it wasn't flying right towards me after all, but just as I was considering the wisdom of dropping to the ground and protecting the back of my neck with my hands, the eagle sailed by, perhaps a wingspan away. It took many minutes of quietly contemplating the six eagles perched indifferently in the Cottonwood at the end of the path for my heart's pounding to slow.

Having seen eagles up close, I wanted to experience them in large numbers. Earlier in November, my river-diving friend Jeff had invited me to see the film *The Heart of the Fraser,* about agricultural threats to the roughly 80 kilometres of critical salmon spawning habitat between Mission and Hope on the Fraser River. This area sustains almost 30 species of fish, including salmon and sturgeon, and in recent years it has been the wintering ground for large numbers of Bald Eagles. I contacted a fish guiding company to see if they offered eagle-watching tours and arranged for a trip in late November.

The words *rapt* and *raptor* come from the same Latin root, meaning "to seize"—an etymology that makes perfect sense to me. I am captivated by raptors—hawks, owls, eagles, falcons. They hold me rapt: their wings, that second when they throw themselves on the air, the way they look at you, *the fact that they look at you*, all stir something wild and visceral inside me as though I also would take flight. In the Bible, Job, the scriptural exemplar of "when bad things happen to good people," accuses God of hunting him like a lion. For me, it is the image of a ground creature hunted from above by a hawk or an owl that is a metaphor for the spiritual life, or the experience of human-divine encounter. Little mouse-me with a completely full life of scurrying, gathering, nest building, all in two dimensions, can be struck (and indeed seized) by this powerful *something* from the air that devastatingly adds another dimension to my flat world. I find watching raptors is so moving, intense, and in some way private, that I hesitated to bring my family to see them.

Yet there we were, a party of four: myself, my partner, Julie, my daughter, Harriet, and her dad, Bruce, host to the crow nest. In the end, it was some combination of frugality and generosity that made my decision. I could not conscience the expense of a boat charter for just myself, and I wanted the people I love to experience some of what I do seeing eagles. We met our guide, a personable young guy who seemed a bit confused that eagles and not fish were our goal, at a riverside park north of Chilliwack. He steered us out onto the water in a small jet boat with a zippered vinyl cover that offered shelter for four, six if you were very close or very small. No one in our family is small, so we moved carefully about the little craft.

The river was wide, muddy brown, and fairly slow-moving. All around us were gravel and grass, with Cottonwood growing on silt flats that flood during the spring freshet; farther back, rocky hills were treed with conifers. As we pushed off from the bank, a single eagle lifted off from the opposite shore, arced towards us across the water and headed upriver. One.

We followed the Fraser briefly west and then curved east, rounding the high and rocky Queens Island. A pair eagles crossed the water ahead of us. Two, Three. To the northeast of the island, we headed up the Harrison River. Where the two rivers met, clear green water flowed into the muddy brown, creating vivid spirals, and the little boat was tossed a bit in eddies and whirlpools.

Past the junction, the Harrison River widens, and in the shadow of high rocks we passed under a railway bridge. In trees along the shore we started to see eagles: dark triangle shapes with bright white heads. Four. Five. Six. Seveneightnine. And then it became apparent that my counting was off, because there were juveniles among the adults, but with their dark heads and splotchier colouring, much harder to spot. Bald Eagles are solitary hunters and they are territorial during mating season, but they will cease hostilities to feed in close proximity to one another when food is abundant, and in winter they can even be quite social.

We approached some kind of log storage area with huge metal pilings standing upright in the water and logs stacked on a manufactured spit and floating near the banks. The closer we got, the more eagles we could see. Twenty-eight. Twenty-nine. Dozens at the water's edge were in a constant state of motion: rising up, jockeying for position, then settling back down again; making short, aggressive hops and dives at each other and the gulls who edged closer and closer in the hope of scavenging from the scavengers. There were eagles perched atop the mountains of logs on the shore, on every other piling, and on floating logs. From the highest point on the stacked logs, an adult eagle slowly turned its glaringly white head, marking our passage.

Eagles' eyesight is four to seven times better than that of humans; they have superior colour vision, seeing both ultraviolet light and more gradations of colour than we do. Their visual acuity is such that they can see a rabbit from five kilometres away: in human terms that would be like seeing the sweat on a performer or an athlete's face from the cheapest seats in the stadium. The placement of Bald Eagles' eyes means that they can see 340 degrees without turning their heads. To the sides, their monocular peripheral vision allows them to detect any movement, and then focus in, like the eagle that was tracking our boat, with acute, three-dimensional binocular vision.

As the eagle watched us float by I said a brief prayer of thanksgiving for the life of Gordon August. Before his death in May 2018, I had worked alongside the Shíshálh (Sechelt) elder and cultural teacher, opposing the expansion of the Trans Mountain pipeline, a project that, in addition to the risks it poses for humans, threatens critical bird habitat. August was known to most of us as Eagle Eyes, a name he had been given after a prolonged vigil, or staring contest, with a Bald Eagle.

Our guide cut the engine, and as the boat drifted toward the floating logs, a few of the eagles rose briefly and settled back down, while others were completely indifferent to us. A mature adult had hauled a huge salmon carcass onto a floating log and was tearing chunks of flesh with its large, curved bill, while grasping the fish's body with its powerful talons. The inside surfaces of a Bald Eagle's talons are covered with tiny spikes to help it grasp prey, particularly slippery fish. I was excited, after learning this, to return to my photographs of the salmon ceremony on the Chilliwack River and discover that these spikes, called spicules, were clearly visible on Eddie Gardner's eagle-claw staff.

We wanted to be close enough to see and not so close that we caused the eagles to fly away. Local First Nations, eagle and salmon conservationists, and other citizen groups have developed a Bald Eagle etiquette guide, asking hikers and kayakers to stay out of the nearby Chehalis Flats Preserve between October and February and to observe the eagles at a distance. Eagles can soar with very little effort, but flapping flight takes energy; in the winter the chief occupation of eagles, many of whom migrate 2,000 to 3,000 kilometres each spring and fall, is to feed, rest, and build up their reserves.

Bald Eagles' peregrinations, so to speak, are complex, and the timing of their mating and nesting depends on location and food availability. While eastern populations have different patterns, the thriving West Coast population's movements are determined for about six months of year by access to salmon remains.

The Fraser Valley is home to more than 500 nesting pairs of Bald Eagles. Additional tens of thousands arrive after flying 1,600 to 2,400 kilometres from the more northern parts of the province, Alaska, and Yukon, as their food supply freezes up. In mid-fall, eagles that breed locally begin to arrive in the region and build or refurbish nests. Eagles tend to nest near the trunk, high up in conifers or Cottonwoods that protrude above the canopy, offering easy flight access and good visibility. Farther south in their range, Bald Eagles will nest in deciduous trees and even cacti. Their nests are incredible, and they return to them year after year; some nests have been continuously occupied for decades, sometimes by subsequent pairs. An eagles' nest can be 10 feet across—or, as I apparently tell my children "all the time"—bigger than our couch. And more impressive than their size is their weight. The largest eagles' nest on record weighed 2,000 kilograms, or two metric tonnes—*more than Volkswagen Beetle!* As part of their pair bonding activity, a pair of eagles can spend months carefully constructing or redecorating a nest, but in the event of an accident they will also throw one together quite hurriedly.

As the cold season advances, the rest of the eagles, immatures and northern breeders, arrive and all the eagles devote the short, cold days to finding food, mostly salmon. In early March, the wintering populations return fairly quickly to their home-territories, rising on thermals, then drifting with the wind, while the locals put some additional polish on their nests and turn their attention to mating.

Bald Eagles engage in courtship behaviour to select a mate and to re-establish their bond when reunited. These behaviours start out large-scale and dramatic: locking talons and spin-falling together towards the ground, chasing one another, and performing steep, repeated dives like a roller coaster; and then they shift to smaller scale and more proximal: nest construction, preening, and simultaneous vocalizations. Copulation occurs on a branch or in the nest. When a female is ready to mate, she calls to her partner and makes bowing motions. The male climbs on her back, they adjust their tails, align their cloacas, and sperm is transferred.

After mating, a pair will fine-tune nest preparations, adding more sticks and lining it with softer materials like grass, moss, and cedar greens. In February through March in the Pacific Northwest, the female lays one to three whitish, tennis ball–sized eggs. The parents take turns incubating the eggs, which hatch 35 days after they were laid. The chicks hatch in a relatively immature or altricial state requiring food and warmth from adults. Both parents supply food, tearing off strips and holding them out to the largest and most demanding chicks' bills. In British Columbia, where food is abundant, as many as three chicks may survive, but where food is scarce and siblings must compete, the smaller, later-born chicks can starve, be killed, or be pushed out of the nest.

Raccoons and Common Ravens are occasional nest predators, but adult Bald Eagles are usually at the top of the food chain, with no natural predators. They are not, however, invincible. A Black Bear, a Grey Wolf, a Red-Tailed Hawk or even a persistent mob of Northwestern Crows may drive an eagle off of a meal, and Great Horned Owls are known to usurp their nests. Occasionally, an adult will be mortally injured in a territorial dispute or by another species, including a case in the summer of 2018 in Maine where a loon fatally stabbed a Bald Eagle in the heart with its dagger-like bill.

By the end of July, juvenile Bald Eagles are fully fledged and appear larger than their parents because they have extra-long flight feathers. In August, the family disperses, with each individual going in different directions. The juveniles itinerate long distances, learning to find food and eventually to hunt on their own, over a period of years. Nesting pairs and newly mature eagles will return in the fall, and the cycle begins again.

Typically, when juveniles reach sexual maturity at age five, signified by the white-head–brown-body plumage, they form a lifelong pair bond, only seeking a new mate if their partner dies or appears to fail at producing viable eggs. But not every Bald Eagle is typical. Sometimes a new pair will not mate in their first year; they may spend some time building a nest, assessing the feeding capacity of their territory, and perhaps evaluating one another as well. One spring in the 1980s, I observed a pair of eagles on Vancouver Island tending a nest where one of the pair had not yet developed adult plumage. There are also several documented cases of one male and two females sharing a nest and raising large clutches together. Two males in Illinois seem to have formed a pair bond. Between 2016 and the time of writing, the males, Valor I and Valor II, have shared a nest and offspring with two consecutive female partners. There are also documented cases of adult Bald Eagle nest helpers who are not parents of the chicks they feed and defend.

Across from the log booms on the Harrison River, a row of 20 eagles sat near the water on a rocky bar; from the far side of the bar we could see another 20 heads, turning to follow the motion of the boat or rising up and down, tearing away at a salmon carcass. From tail to bill, a Bald Eagle is about 70 centimetres tall, which means that a small male could walk under a dining room table without brushing his head, and a large female could pull a salmon cutlet off a kitchen counter. In low trees across the water, there were more eagles. My count was over 100, but at that point, with so many birds, I was guessing a bit.

We continued upriver under a car bridge, and our guide described the challenges of bringing big boats up to Harrison Lake: you want water high enough that the boats can make the trip without scraping bottom, but high water can put the top of a craft dangerously close to the underside of bridges.

By a golf course on the north side of the river and along the water's edge, a few dozen eagles were feeding, their bright yellow feet clearly visible. As we cut our engine to watch, one rose up and flapped slowly towards us. It crossed close behind our boat, the salmon head in its talons trailing about a metre of spine. On the south shore, trees on the bank were full of eagles. In the bare deciduous trees they were easy to see in silhouette: on one huge limb I counted six individuals. In the evergreen fir and cedar, they were harder to spot, particularly the juveniles.

We started the engine again and continued upriver, passing many trees with as many as 10 to 12 individuals in each one, and my counting turned to multiplication: seven trees times 10 eagles is 70. Somewhere in the low 300s I stopped trying to keep track and declared that there were, indeed, "more eagles than I have ever seen at one time."

A gathering of eagles is sometimes mistakenly called an *aerie*, but that is the term for an eagles' nest. A *cast* of hawks refers to birds released by a falconer, so it could apply to eagles should one happen to be hawking with a group of emperors, but it is probably not the best term for everyday use. In the *Chronicles of Narnia*, C.S. Lewis borrowed from Chaucer's allegorical poem *The Parliament of Fowls*, where all birds convene to choose mates. Lewis used *parliament* to describe a council meeting of owls, to such advantage that, despite the complete lack of historical precedent, *parliament* has become the modern collective for owls. Although the term is occasionally extended to eagles, I hesitate to infringe on Lewis' linguistic coup. What, then, to call this gathering of eagles? I have not been able to trace the origins of the modern collective *convocation* for eagles, but the word itself, derived from Latin via the French, means "a calling or coming together, often ecclesial or academic," so, as a priest with scholarly aspirations who seeks out the company of eagles, it seems to me an entirely a fitting name.

Let me take you on another engaging detour. As I researched collective terms for eagles, I learned that the word *aquiline*, which I had always thought meant "striking" and had never encountered describing anything besides a human profile, actually means "eagle-like." More excitingly, I learned that words like aquiline, canine, bovine, and porcine are called "collateral adjectives"—descriptors associated with a particular noun, (eagle, dog, cow, and pig respectively) but not derived from it.

And now, back to the river. At the place where the Chehalis River enters the Harrison, there is a kind of breakwater where a dozen eagles were perched on wooden pilings. The alluvial fan where the rivers meet is a critical habitat for salmon, and, in winter, as many as 15,000 eagles congregate to feast on spawned-out salmon carcasses. Keeping to the deep channel on the south, we could see eagles in on both sides of the river. A little farther upriver, we passed the mouth of Weaver Creek, where a few late-spawning salmon would be making their way.

Closer to Harrison Lake, as the banks of the river got steeper, there were fewer eagles, so we looped back downriver and stopped for lunch on a rocky bar across from the Chehalis flats. The weather was shifting between cloud and sun, and occasional drops of rain would splatter the plastic windows of the boat. I was grateful that our picnic thermoses included hot drinks with a shot of whiskey.

Our guide nosed the little boat up against the shore and jumped out, pulling a chain and anchor behind him. We clambered over the bow, found semi-private places to pee in the bush, and walked on a gravel bar, too cold to stand still for long. The ground was littered with fallen leaves and the bodies hundreds of salmon; I crouched down for a closer look. Most were leering heads, all hooked jaws, sharp teeth, and empty sockets, with the bones stripped bare. And, although I couldn't tell the species apart, the differences in size were striking. When I stood up I saw that the Cottonwood leaf that had blown up against my boot was in fact a soft brown eagle's feather.

Dame Juliana did not leave us a collective noun for salmon, but she did not completely ignore them. The first item in her list of proper terms for butchering or dressing "fysshes" is "a sawmon chyned" or "a salmon spined," and with their bones picked bare, the salmon on the rock island seemed to have been thoroughly chyned. As we crunched through the rocks, live salmon jumped in the shallow water, and the river bottom was littered with rotting bodies. Between the bar and the shore, a pair of faded red and green Sockeye were moving as though ready to spawn, but a trout was marking them closely—darting in repeatedly. Our guide said it was feeding on eggs.

As I looked into trees on the shore, I could see several nearby stands where eight or 10 eagles were sitting. A few moved from one tree to another, some flying off and others landing, unperturbed by our presence. As I stared longer into the dense greens of the trees, more and more individuals, especially juveniles, seem to emerge from the background—in the shadow of the trunk, partially concealed by a branch, facing away from the water. As my eyes drifted upwards I realized that there were eagles not just in the trees nearest the shore but in the trees behind those and higher up the hill as well. Whatever my eagle count was, I needed to multiply it by three at least.

Our guide had rhapsodized a bit about how quiet the river was, but he must have been referring to the number of boats on the water, because he had to shout over the sound of the little craft's engine. On the bar it was quieter, but far from silent: the water made a rushing sound, leaping salmon smacked against its surface, a small flock of Glaucuous-winged Gulls bobbed on the water, screaming into each others' faces, and audible over all of that was the piping call of the eagles. The Bald Eagle's call is described in field guides and on nature websites in less than laudatory terms: weak-sounding, thin and squeaky, a high whinny. Often, in movies, the Red-Tailed Hawk's hoarse screeching *keee-year* is dubbed in for an eagle. To me, the eerie, fluting call of the Bald Eagle is quite stirring, and those who find it disappointing remind me of the woman who could only see photographers blocking her driveway and not the eagle on her roof. When we have expectations for what the Sacred will be like, we can fail to recognize it when it shows up.

As our family drifted towards one another and convened on the south side of the gravel bar, a brief shower of rain passed over and a fat, sturdy rainbow appeared across the river. Our attention shifted between sky, trees, and water.

In the trees above the gulls, a group of perhaps 10 eagles began to vocalize more insistently, maybe responding to the gulls, maybe to one another; then there seemed to be a shift in energy or attention. One of the eagles made a short flight of perhaps two hundred metres past our viewpoint to another very full tree; its landing resulted in a swelling of voices and some adjustment of positions within the tree. In a few minutes, a second eagle followed, landing in the same clump of trees, and after that a third. Each approach and landing involved calling back and forth between the bird in the air and those in the tree, and then a small cascade of shuffling on branches and displacement within the tree. A dislodged immature eagle launched into the air and began circling overhead. Over about ten minutes, more and more eagles took to the air, spiraling above us in lazy circles, calling back and forth. It was nothing like the flocking behaviour of geese or even the crows, but certainly they were reading each other's movements and responding to one another in this collective action.

Then two of the birds began to engage in a spectacular display, shrieking and diving at one another, talons extended. They grappled in mid-air, pinwheeled for two full rotations, and then chased each other across the fading rainbow.

This behavior, characteristic of courting eagles, is also exhibited by non-mating birds in territory disputes. Often in the winter or spring, an eagle will lock its talons into another's feet or flesh and both will fall to the ground. The Orphaned Wildlife Rehabilitation Society (OWL), the local wildlife sanctuary specializing in raptors, frequently responds to such incidents, often separating the birds and allowing them to fly away, other times treating their injuries. These natural encounters differ from the majority of calls to the raptor centre, where birds have been harmed by human action: shooting, becoming entangled in ropes, net, or fishing line, or poisoning from consuming animals whose bodies contain lead shot or rodent poison.

Whether they were galvanized by the sparring eagles in the air or some critical mass had been reached, more and more eagles abandoned their perches until there were easily 50 eagles circling above us and spiraling upward. This was the moment that we all remarked on after.

Making our way back to our launching place, we passed under the bridges and marveled again at the line where the green waters of the Harrison met the muddy brown of the Fraser. In the shadow of a small island, a large rock really, we spotted a seal. The current carried us away, but looking over our shoulders, we could see two more seals hauling their leopard-patterned backs high out of the water as they made rolling dives.

They were unafraid and curious; one paused and looked straight at us, the head and tail of a salmon dangling from either side of its mouth like a comic moustache. Like the eagles, seals follow the salmon runs miles up the river from the ocean. These seals were about 120 kilometres from the ocean; they are regular visitors to Harrison Lake and even farther upriver. In Oregon, California Sea Lions swim as far as Wilamette Falls in pursuit of salmon. In the United States, culling of seals and sea lions that prey on fish in rivers has been proposed to increase salmon numbers, but that is a "quick fix" that does not require any change in human overfishing and habitat destruction.

At the end of the day, as we unloaded thermoses, binoculars, and jackets, feet a bit unsteady on the shore, I stopped to reflect. Watching 50 eagles circling above my little family had made my heart beat fast and my chest feel like something big and good was swelling inside me. But it was not their numbers that had impressed me. More than any other large group I had encountered, I found I was taken with the eagles as individuals, with their immense size. In thinking back on the day, my head was filled with the details of their connection to and place within a complex ecosystem. I was seeing not just Bald Eagles but their web of relationships to salmon, herons, crows, sea mammals, the river, the trees, the ocean, and even me.

Animals of the Salish Sea: Coast Salish First Nations and Native Art

By Melaney Gleeson-Lyall

Garfinkel, 2016

This beautiful board book, featuring the artwork of 13 Coast Salish artists, shares information and cultural teaching about 26 animals that live in and around the Salish Sea.

Fraser Valley Bald Eagle Festival

A volunteer-run free weekend festival in November between Mission and Harrison Mills. Tours and activities celebrate the return of overwintering Bald Eagles. The website has information year-round.

fraservalleybaldeaglefestival.ca

Hancock Wildlife Foundation

The foundation's mission is to promote the conservation and appreciation of wildlife and their habitats through programs that include consultation, publication, research, and public engagement. The website has links to live cams and has some of the most comprehensive material on Bald Eagles available online.

hancockwildlife.org

The Heart of the Fraser

By Ken Ashley

Moving Images, 2019

This documentary film introduces the Gravel Reach of the Fraser River between Mission and Hope, highlighting its critical ecological importance for spawning Pacific Salmon and White Sturgeon.

OWL (Orphaned Wildlife) Rehabilitation Society

3800-72nd Street, Delta, BC, Canada
OWL is a nonprofit organization dedicated to the rescue, rehabilitation, and release of injured and orphaned raptors and to public education on raptor conservation. They are available 24/7 for raptor rescue in the Lower Mainland. Their website has tons of information. They send ambassador birds and humans out to schools and community events, and they welcome visitors on-site.
owlrehab.org

Silent Spring

By Rachel Carson
Houghton Mifflin, 1962
This book ushered in an era of conservation and is widely considered to be the most important environmental book of the 20th century. Carson documented and made public the harms that indiscriminate use of pesticides and herbicides cause to humans and non-humans.

A Raft of Ducks

10

The weather grew colder and the sky was full of wings and great birds flying. From East to West, from North to South, and as far up into the blue sky as eyes could see, were birds and birds and birds sailing on beating wings.

At evening down they came endlessly from the sky, sliding down long slopes of air to rest on the water of Silver Lake.

There were great, gray geese. There were smaller, snow-white brant that looked like snow at the water's edge. There were ducks of many kinds, the large mallards with a shimmering of purple and green on their wings, the redheads, the bluebills, the canvasbacks, and teals and many others whose names Pa did not know.

Laura Ingalls Wilder, 1913

This year did not follow the measured pace that I had imagined: a visit to one large gathering of creatures each month. There was a relative dearth of congregating creatures in the late spring and summer, and then the fall and winter months were filled with activity. Before I gave in and let the creatures dictate the pace, I kept trying to organize chapters around the calendar. My strategy to include all the winter activity was to sneak in extra dates and liturgical seasons from the church calendar in addition to the months of the year: between November 1 and January 6, I thought about a chapter for All Souls Day, New Year's Day, Epiphany, and each of November, December, and January. This would have been the chapter for Advent.

In the western Christian calendar, Advent begins on the fourth Sunday before Christmas. The season has become commercialized since I was a child and a chocolate Advent calendar was a rare treat (or maybe I was just sheltered). Today, chocolate is the baseline. Playmobil offers a 24-figure plastic nativity set, there are jewelry calendars with four-figure price tags, and it is possible that my spouse lugged home a calendar containing not quite 20 litres of craft beer on public transit. Calendar excesses not withstanding, Advent was traditionally an austere season of solemn anticipation, sometimes compared with the fasting and penitence of Lent. The assigned scripture passages are heavy on John the Baptist and "you brood of vipers!" My favorite symbol for marking this passage of days while we wait for something sacred to be born is the quasi-pagan Advent wreath. A wheel of evergreens is brought indoors and illuminated with another candle each week, until on Christmas Eve the Christ candle in the centre is lit, and the whole thing is a circle of light and boughs that stay green in winter.

During the second week of Advent, I returned to Boundary Bay determined to spend time with the shorebirds. But Advent is a tricky season. Part of the point of Bethlehem, the mighty king born in a manger, and angels visiting shepherds (of all people) is that the Sacred shows up in unexpected ways. Advent is a time to practice expecting the unexpected.

Shorebirds are mudflat and intertidal foragers who can also live inland; most have small, teardrop-shaped bodies with long bills and legs. Examples include many sandpiper species, dowitchers, and curlews, all in various shades of speckled brown, and the singular-looking Black Oystercatchers, with their red-orange bills. Nearly 30 species, many distinguished by subtle differences in bill or wing length, utilize the shoreline off the city of Richmond between Boundary Bay and Westham Island. It is a major stop on the Pacific Flyway, one of four major migratory routes for birds between their wintering grounds in South America and summer breeding territory in the Arctic. At least a billion birds each year migrate all or part of this 6,000-kilometre route, with tiny shorebirds travelling some of the longest distances. According to a 2014 study by Environment Canada and Birds Canada, the entire Pacific Flyway population of Western Sandpipers and Dunlin can be found on the Fraser River delta during migration. In the same area where Pacific Salmon are acclimating to salt water, several million shorebirds stop each year during their migration, and tens of thousands of them remain for the winter.

Since the publication of Rachael Carson's *Silent Spring* raised the alarm, some waterfowl, like the Lesser Snow Goose, and raptors, like the Bald Eagle, have made impressive recoveries, but globally, bird populations have declined in almost every habitat. Studies utilizing data from bird watchers and citizen scientists have documented a 29 percent reduction in the number of birds in Canada and the US since 1970. Shorebird populations have been particularly hard-hit, losing an estimated 70 percent of their previous numbers. The impacts of climate change on their Arctic breeding grounds are a major cause of decline, as is shoreline development. Boundary Bay is part of a globally designated "Important Bird Area" and the most immediate threat to this critical shorebird habitat is a proposed expansion to the Roberts Bank shipping terminal. The mega-project includes a new three-berth container terminal and expanding the existing causeway across 177 hectares of the Fraser River estuary, which would disrupt water currents and flow patterns, damaging a vital food source for the birds. On the intertidal mudflats, Western Sandpipers fuel up for a 1,000-kilometre leg of their migratory journey by consuming a slimy biofilm, rich in microscopic algae.

When we see thousands of shorebirds, the tens of thousands that we no longer see are hard to imagine. The benefits of port expansion are tangible and quantifiable, while the benefits and meaning of an at least somewhat intact ecosystem are hard to know. What does a billion even look like? Do we actually *need* a billion birds?

It is easy to think that large numbers are inexhaustible or will always be there. This is what our forbears thought about the Passenger Pigeon; it is how we are treating forests and oceans, and so it was for me and the shorebirds and this book. In the early part of the year, the excitement of sea lions, charismatic macro-fauna, as they say, and the familiarity of the East Van crows took precedence. There would plenty of time to see shorebirds; there were so many of them, and they were always there. If I missed them during their northward migration, I could catch them in the fall heading south. Since October, I had seen clouds of shorebirds along the water's edge on several occasions, but this December day I was determined to finally have a chapter-worthy encounter with thousands or tens of thousands.

When I arrived at the park, I could see at least a dozen Bald Eagles perched in bare deciduous trees, Poplars, I think. A pair near the parking lot looked impossibly huge. As I was staring up at them, a jewel-bright Anna's Hummingbird zipped across my line of sight. At one-twentieth of the eagles' wingspan and one-thousandth of their weight (somewhere between a nickel and a quarter) they made a perfect study in contrasts. Voted Vancouver's official city bird in 2017, Anna's Hummingbirds are a recent year-rounder, first appearing in the 2005 Christmas bird count. With warmer winters, the popularity of more "exotic" garden vegetation, and a ready supply of year-round, sugar-water filled plastic feeders, the versatile Anna's have made the Lower Mainland home, supplementing their diet of nectar with insects and periodically entering a torpor state during the cold months. At the other extreme, Bald Eagle bones have been found in shell middens over 1,000 years old, and their co-existence with humans in this region is likely thousands of years longer.

I headed towards the beach where I had seen shorebirds in late October. On the way, I passed a small pond full of waterfowl, mostly Mallards, Canada Geese, and various gulls. Three Bald Eagles perched in trees over the pond, one immature swiveling its head back and forth was clearly tracking the movements of the swimmers below. Although they appeared oblivious, waterfowl often rotate sentry duty, with one or two keeping watch for predators while the others feed.

The tide was much closer-in than at my last visit, and there were shorebirds on the sand in two clusters of about 100 each. Little brown birds on stilt-like legs thrusting about in the wet sand, busily feeding and peeping. I guessed that they were Western Sandpipers, not because I am any good at identifying shorebirds, but because they were the most statistically likely. Not seeing the thousands of birds I had hoped for, I drifted north beside the water, first on the path and then out onto a sand bar that runs parallel with the shore, creating a little inlet within the bay.

As I walked, occasional clouds of shore birds, 30 to 50 in number, would sweep along the water's edge, forming and reforming. Boomerang-shaped wings all turning together in tight formation, the flash of their light-coloured underparts was like a swivel billboard revealing a new image. This synchronized motion is called a *murmuration*. The word first appeared in the *Boke of Seynt Albans* as the company term for a group of starlings. "A Murmuracion of Stares," likely referred to the birds' noisy chatter, but it has come to describe the swirling, coordinated flocking motion of any group of small birds in flight.

Their movement was fascinating, but the shorebirds in their see-through cloud seemed ephemeral compared with the ponderous mass of ducks. There were hundreds of them. In the little inlet, out on the water of the bay, in the reeds at the water's edge: Shovelers with their enormous heavy bills, Widgeons, Mallards, Golden-Eyes, tiny Green-Winged Teal, their name shining in the low light.

A word about vocabulary here. *Shorebirds* are the little water's-edge foragers; most don't swim. *Seabirds*, including gulls, loons, and cormorants, live, feed, and breed partially or entirely at sea and are often long-winged fliers and excellent divers. *Waterfowl* refers to ducks, geese, and swans, which can live in fresh or salt water, have sturdy, buoyant bodies, long necks, and webbed feet. Shorebirds, seabirds, and waterfowl all congregate on Boundary Bay in great numbers, and while all were present, it was the waterfowl that clamored for my attention.

And they *were* clamoring. The quote from Laura Ingalls Wilder at the top of the chapter continues, "the whole large lake was covered with birds speaking in every kind of bird's voice to each other before they went to sleep for a night." Like that Dakota lake, Boundary Bay was noisy with "every kind of bird's voice." Widgeons, a medium-sized duck with a pale blue bill and a white forehead blaze on the males, whistled incessantly. Teals made shrill conversational chatter back and forth, and the Shovelers emitted a honking kind of "chok-chock." All of these were drowned out by the intermittent, harsh "wack, wack, wack," of the Mallards. Its shiny, green head, curly black tail, and adaptability to urban environments make this ancestor of almost all domestic breeds perhaps the best-known duck in the world. I am convinced that the cranky cartoon characters Donald and Daffy Duck both take their inspiration from the Mallard's impatient-sounding series of stereotypical quacks. The joke is on Disney and Warner Brothers, however, if gender matters, since it is only the female that makes this call.

As I walked, a dozen larger, white-rumped ducks flushed and flew off at such an angle that all I could really see was their butts. A few minutes later, I startled a lone (poor thing) Snow Goose, which erupted from the grass behind me. It made a single loud cry of alarm; its feet slapped on the ground as it ran, and its wings hissed against the dried grass, but its launch into the air was completely silent, so different from the shattering sound of the flock, or gaggle, I had encountered in November.

Obviously my walking was causing the birds to take flight, so I stretched out on the cold sand between two cedar logs bleached, hairy and fibrous. They formed a natural blind where I could turn my head one way to watch the floating waterfowl drifting out on the bay and the other to see a much smaller group busily feeding in the little inlet.

I pulled out my binoculars to focus on the ducks at the edges of the inlet and realized that, mottled brown and camouflaged among the vegetation on the margin, there were nearly as many ducks bedded down on the shore as there were in the water. Alone among the ducks, I spied a single Brant, a small, dark goose with a white band at its throat, and I realized that what I had taken for white-rumped ducks earlier were in fact Brant. Across the inlet, a line of low trees and bushes was dotted with raptors, Bald Eagles, Northern Harriers, and one little accipiter, either a Cooper's or a Sharp-Shinned Hawk. A beautiful Short-Eared Owl was hunting in the grass, the dark markings at its eyes and wrists striking against its pale underside. There was so much going on, I could not decide where to focus my attention.

Swiveling back to the bay, I spied a pair of Pacific Loons low in the water, sporting their coastal winter-mist colours of charcoal and soft grey. The bird closer to me had a flat fish the size of a tea saucer grasped in its bill and was slapping it vigorously against the surface of the water.

I scanned out over the floating waterfowl, trying to identify species: Wigeons—a lot of Wigeons—Mallards, Brant, Shovelers. What's that black and white, a lot of black and white? Goldeneye? Ring-Necked Duck? Scaup?

Because waterfowl have been both hunted and farmed, there is a wealth of vocabulary to refer to them in groups: the already mentioned plump and gaggle of geese, a *herd* of swans, a *covert* of Coots and the evocative, if mysterious, *sword* of Mallards. Ducks and geese in the air can both be referred to as a *skein* or a *wedge*. Dame Juliana calls a group of "Dokis" a "badelyng" or "paddling," a term that best suits those colourful ducks foraging in the inlet. In fact, ducks are subdivided into *dabblers*, with bright heads and wing-patches who feed on invertebrates and vegetation at the surface or tip their butts in the air to go a little deeper, and *divers,* who submerge completely in pursuit of mollusks and fish and have a colour-scheme similar to a black and white police cruiser. The large numbers out on the bay included mostly divers. *Raft* is the company term for a large number of ducks floating together and an excellent descriptor for the flotillas of diving ducks drifting on the bay.

Looking across the water toward where the Little Campbell River (of the toad migration and salmon hatchery) empties into the bay, I tried to get some sort of count, an estimate of the numbers I was looking at.

"Okay, so if that near group is maybe 15 deep and 30 long, that's 450, so if I round up for stragglers that's 500. Now multiply that by the number of groups: I count four, five, six. Okay, that's 3,000 but there's clearly another raft behind that."

I raised my binoculars a little and realized, *crap!* The shimmering white behind the second great raft of ducks was not light reflecting off the surface of the water, but thousands of Snow Geese, and the darker strands among them were more bay ducks and Brant. Tens of thousands of floating birds, stretching away further than my eye, or even my binoculars, could distinguish. They weren't up close or interacting with me in any way, but I was quietly astounded by their presence. From the placid footballs bobbing a few metres away to the specks of glitter on the horizon, each was a real and solid, beaky, noisy eating-machine that had traveled farther in a year than I ever would.

As their coastal habitats are developed for industry, agriculture, and human habitation, global shorebird numbers are in decline, but many species of waterfowl have rebounded tremendously. In Canada and the United States, a contributing factor in this resurgence is the work of recreational hunters, who through organizations like Ducks Unlimited have organized, funded, and lobbied for intensive wetland conservation. Even more important is the North American Waterfowl Management Plan. The tri-national agreement, conceived when waterfowl numbers were at historic lows in the 1980s, is the most successful wildlife plan in North America and has contributed to significant increases in most waterfowl species. Thanks to these conservation efforts, a staggering eight million waterfowl pass through the coastal areas of Vancouver Island and the Lower Mainland during winter migration.

I passed a delightful hour switching my attention back and forth between the bay and the inlet. Intermittent drifts of Sandpipers zigzagged along the shoreline. At one point, a mature Bald Eagle dislodged itself from a bare tree, crossed over where I lay and flew out across the bay. It razed the glittering white raft of birds on the water, and an enormous cloud of geese billowed up and settled again, too far away even to hear. I had been idly tracking the progress of the Pacific Loons in the foreground while giving most of my attention to the birds out on the water when I realized that one of them had been a particularly long time with its head-end under water—odd for a diver. I trained my binoculars on the grey, triangular duck-butt to find myself looking directly into the eyes of a seal.

The winter solstice was drawing near, with sunset around 4:15, fully five hours earlier than in July, when I had waited for the Burvilla bats to emerge. By mid-afternoon the light had begun to fade, and as I walked back along the ridge of the sandy spit, I discovered a bone-yard of bleached remains. Flattened vegetation lay in dried circles of leafless greys and browns, interspersed with not just the usual beach leavings of crab claws and bivalve shells, but washed-up trees, roots and all; a large gull's wing intact all the way to the scapular; a half-metre circle of large, drab tail and primary feathers; a lone white pencil-thin bone a hand span long (gleeful poring over internet images later revealed it to be a radius, probably from a duck or small goose); a drift of the softest down coloured grey, cream, and rust; a fused segment of fish spine. It appeared that the park raptors were eating well.

At the southernmost end of the little inlet, where the sand spit met the shore, the ducks seemed to have been stirred into swirls of agitation. As I watched, the frantic calling and dashing about resolved into a pattern: one duck was swimming about in distress, calling loudly and creating a ripple of responses from others wherever it went. The duck, a female Shoveler, would dart forward and then begin to spin in circles, sometimes going completely under water before righting itself and darting forward again. I watched for five or 10 minutes thinking ... I don't know what, that the situation might somehow resolve itself?

I assumed the duck had an injured leg, and I wondered if it had been attacked by one of the raptors. Harriers will take a Teal, but the more likely predator for a duck of that size would be a Bald Eagle. Sub-adults take significant time to develop their hunting skills, so a failed strike is a common occurrence.

I approached the water's edge and all the ducks, including the injured Shoveler, moved quickly away. Clearly, my half-formed plan of flopping my coat over this duck, popping her in a milk crate from my trunk and whisking her off to a rescue centre was not going to happen. I called the Orphaned Wildlife Rehabilitation Society just 15 minutes away around the bay and got a sympathetic volunteer on the phone, but was unsurprised to learn that they are only able to come out to rescue trapped or injured raptors. While it is a great thing that waterfowl numbers are in resurgence and that there are rescue teams ready to mobilize for birds of prey, if you are an injured, middle-of-the-food-chain, one duck in eight million, nature is allowed to take its course.

During our current era of extinctions, in a year of proximity to tens of thousands of creatures, it is surprising that I had not seen more death. As darkness began to fall on the very end of this full, strange year I left behind the not-long-for-this-world duck and trudged away over the sand, crunching shells and bones beneath my feet.

On the drive home, I counted more than 70 Bald Eagles on trees and transmission towers near the landfill, and then, driving north through the city, I caught the tail-end of the East Van crows' nightly sojourn, groups of 50 and 100 winging east overhead. I reflected back on this year of encounters, starting with the Salmon Ceremony on the Vedder River: 400 Great Blue Herons, 1,000 California Sea Lions, 10,000 Snow Geese, and various and sundry crows, bats, toads, moths, salmon, eagles, and ducks and the accompanying hawks, bear, owls, Common Ravens, Western Red Cedar, ferns, and mosquitos.

I had begun with a loosely held question about interspecies loneliness: Am I different? Or how am I different, because I do not have regular encounters or casual proximity to large numbers of creatures? How might I, and by implication other first-world, North American, urban humans, be changed if we spent more time in the company of our creature companions? Real life is full of plot holes and narrative cul-de-sacs, and this year of encounters did not exhibit the rising action, climax, and tidy denouement of a novel. But there were patterns to this patchwork year of animal aggregations and, I hope, wisdom gained.

Initially, I thought that the important part of this project was happening "in the field," in each direct encounter with the gaggle, or knot, or colony of the moment, and that the rest was just paperwork. But I discovered that much of the weight, meaning, and deeper resonance of an experience happened afterwards. It was not simply documenting, "What happened and what did I notice?" but rather in asking, "What did I learn? What more do I need to know?" and, "How can I communicate the heart of this?" that the experience was fully realized. I saw patterns and filled in blanks that I had not known were there.

There is a strong parallel here to intentional spiritual practice. From time to time I have participated in retreats in the rather rigorous tradition of the Spiritual Exercises of St. Ignatius of Loyola: days of mostly silence, where participants alternate between periods of prayer and times of reflection on that prayer—noticing patterns and asking questions. It is almost always in the consideration of the raw experience that moments of realization happen.

Much of what I gained over the course of this year was information, which for me is a kind of treasure. I often express my love and enthusiasm through study. Indeed the word *amateur* comes from the Latin for lover. For me, that deep and rigorous engagement with a subject is a form of prayer. In this year of observation and reflection, I acquired not only thrilling statistics—clutch size, wingspan, breeding population, weird sex facts, and adolescent-pleasing grotesqueries—but new ideas.

Before starting this project, I was aware of white-nose syndrome in bats, piscine reovirus in salmon, and that a mysterious "something" was killing off large numbers of amphibians, but I had not thought much at all about the extent to which disease is a regulator of populations, a vehicle for large extinction events, and a significant way in which climate change is expressed.

I learned that abundance does not have a single meaning; it can be an anomaly, a remnant, a monoculture, a success dependent on others' loss. I was aware of the phenomenon of introduced invasive species like European Starlings, American Bullfrogs, and European Wall Lizards, which, in a new habitat without the predators they evolved alongside, will aggressively out-compete native species. Thinking of these a bit like villains in the story, bullies and colonizers, I deliberately avoided these species in my year-long exploration. I was also painfully aware that we are in an era of large-scale extinctions, so I approached some of these encounters with some faintly creepy and voyeuristic ideas, as though this was a "last chance" to experience "vanishing wonders." What I found and hadn't anticipated at all, was that even in a time of mass extinctions there are species that adapt and thrive. The Lesser Snow Geese, California Sea Lions, and Northwestern Crows in particular are favoured by the current constellation of urbanization, conservation efforts, agriculture, and even changing climate. Their perhaps temporary (and really, every species' success is temporary), adaptive success contributes to a phenomenon that is evident particularly in comparatively biomass-dense regions like the Fraser River estuary: climate crisis and ecological disaster can *look* lush and green and teeming even when an ecosystem is critically impoverished.

For those of us raised on television and other instant forms of gratification, it is easy to think about the natural world, the plants and creatures outside the window, as somewhat static, constantly available, waiting for the on-off switch of our attention. But this is not so. Many of these mass gatherings would have been easy to overlook: the Western Toads were a near-miss because I waited too long after the rain, the Yuma and Little Brown Bats were incredibly subtle, and even the rafts of ducks and geese on Boundary Bay would have been unremarkable and perhaps unnoticed if I had stuck to the path on the dunes. So I learned something about seeking and searching. For a significant part of each year, many of the creatures I visited are also absent in some way—dormant, migrated, or waiting to be born. Others congregate visibly only at dawn or sunset. This attending to the interplay between planetary and meteorological rhythms and species' responses was an expected gift of this project, a deepening of my literacy in the language of the watershed where I live.

I am someone who in most social situations tends towards reserve. I don't like to emote publicly and I prefer to examine my own reactions before allowing others access, but being present with large numbers of animals affected my emotions. In many of these "big number" encounters—actual tons of sea lions throwing themselves from the rocks and smashing into the water, countless Snow Geese lifting off at once all around me—I experienced joy that did not require, or perhaps would not allow, my usual logical override. Sometimes this joy felt like my own physiological herd response, a wild affinity or an unfiltered internal, "Yes, here we go, when the collective moves, I move too!" Other times I experienced more of a fierce exultation, an observer's delight in the profound rightness of each creature: the very satisfying toadness of toads, the fleshy abundance of sea lions, the whirling chaos of moths.

The times when I fell into a deep, wordless attention to the creatures around me, I felt a reverence and respect for the detail and intricacy of individuals, for their complex corporate identity and behaviour, and their drive for survival. Another way of thinking about this is the idea of sacrament. I am old enough to have memorized a catechism in preparation for confirmation and was taught that a sacrament is "an outward and visible sign of an inward and spiritual grace," that is, a tangible experience when something holy happens. For example, the sense of being caught up in a flock of ascending geese. The official (church-sanctioned) sacraments are not a means of making the sacred happen or coercing the Divine, but rather a kind of curated and reliable way to place ourselves in the way of divine encounter. The "outward and visible" parts—water on the head, speaking vows—are not inherently magical, but they become sacraments because of our attention to them; while the Mystery or the Sacred that shows up remains profoundly free and unharnessable. We have sacraments because if we keep putting ourselves in its way, in these postures of attention and waiting—cupping our hands for bread, scanning the sky for the shape of wings, shifting focus so that toads seem to emerge from the gravel— when the Sacred shows up, we are more likely to notice.

Standing under an endless stream of crows and witnessing the sinuous strength of salmon, I was humbled by an awareness of a great unifying force outside of me. The birds and the fish were part of and responding to something larger than either myself or themselves. My access and proximity to this force, through them, reminded me of my very small place in the world. It emphasized my own insignificance, a sense echoed less happily by my inability to help the injured Shoveler.

In none of these encounters with flocks and gaggles and rafts did I experience emotional closeness. These were not the kind of relational or intimate experiences of communion between myself and a single individual that I have sometimes known. So the answer to the question about loneliness, a state to which I admit I am somewhat dispositionally attuned, is both a no and a yes. My loneliness was not reduced by seeking out animal companions in large numbers, but I was in some way comforted.

My ecological grief was met not with a reassurance that everything will be alright—because it absolutely will not be—but it was met. It was met with heat and motion and cries, shit and spit and wings, so many kinds of wings—the membranous wings of bats, the cobwebby wings of moths, the thundering wings of geese, and empty skeleton wings embracing the sand. Imperiled life fiercely living, no matter how humans threaten their survival.

And the emotions I experienced most often and lastingly in this year, joy, humility, and awe, I think make me a better agent for serving that life-force. They are tools that benefit not just me, but other white

North American humans who would seek to do the work of defending and sustaining the kind of ecosystems we have known on this planet in recent millennia, particularly alongside Indigenous communities, whose relationships to and displacement from the land puts them at the forefront of these struggles.

In thinking about this project, I had imagined that these wild encounters would be like a sentimental last glimpse of a vanishing past when the waters teemed, plains thundered, and skies roiled. But instead I repeatedly experienced a profound offering of my attention to a real and contested present where abundance and flourishing exist alongside irreparable loss and extinction.

Arriving home, I added the bleached wing bone to the heron's egg, eagle feather, and salmon vertebra already among the green boughs of our Advent wreath, candlelight reflected off the dark table.

SOURCES AND RESOURCES

Aliens Among Us: Invasive Animals and Plants in British Columbia

By Alex Van Tol, illustrated by Mike Deas

Royal BC Museum Publications, 2015

This entertaining introduction to more than 50 plants and animals that have established themselves in British Columbia is illustrated with photographs and cartoon drawings. Readable for middle-schoolers to adults.

Ducks Unlimited

An 80 year-old organization started by hunters to preserve wetlands and associated habitat of waterfowl through partnerships with various stakeholders. Their website contains media and resources for conservation and education.

ducks.ca

"How a Flock of Birds Can Fly and Move Together"

By Peter Friederici

Audubon Magazine, March-April, 2009

This article for lay readers describes both the thrill and the science of birds' coordinated movement in flight.

North American Ducks, Geese and Swans Identification Guide

By Frank S. Todd

Hancock House, 2018

This detailed photographic field guide includes range maps, illustrations and descriptions. It is the posthumously published work of a noted wildlife photographer and conservationist.

North American Waterfowl Management Plan

An agreement between Canada, the United States and Mexico that conserves and protects wetland and upland habitats, and associated waterfowl populations. Their website has information and publications.

nawmp.wetlandnetwork.ca

"Silent Skies: Billions of North American Birds Have Vanished"

By Jim Daley
Scientific American, September 19, 2019
A short, clear article summarizing recent trends in the overall decline of birds in North America.

"Slime, Shorebirds and Scientific Mystery"

By Daniel Wood
Hakai Magazine, November 15, 2016
An accessible piece of journalism describing Bob Elner's research on Western Sandpipers and the threat to their food systems posed by the proposed Roberts Bank port expansion. Written for *Hakai Magazine*, the online journal of coastal science, the article is also available as a podcast.

WILDLIFE CONGREGATIONS

A Shoal of Anchovies

An Unexpected Chapter or Perhaps an Epilogue

When he had finished speaking, Jesus said to Simon, 'Put out into the deep water and let down your nets for a catch.' Simon answered, 'Master, we have worked all night long but have caught nothing. Yet if you say so, I will let down the nets.' When they had done this, they caught so many fish that their nets were beginning to break. So they signaled to their partners in the other boat to come and help them. And they came and filled both boats, so that they began to sink.

The Gospel of Luke 5:4-7, New Revised Standard Version

The beach was a blanket of silver; 10,000 tiny corpses formed a metre-wide band along the shore, and the roiling water and cloudy sky were shades of pewter and grey.

Between Christmas and New Year's Eve, the regular passage of days is suspended for me. After Boxing Day, when certain traditions involving the consumption of mince tarts and the acquisition of accordion-themed ceramic knickknacks have been observed, everything becomes a blur of food and family, puzzles, books, and the intermittent but urgent need to escape the house and its occupants.

I thought that with the Advent chapter and the rafts of ducks this book was finished, my year of animal aggregations complete. But I was surprised by one last station on this pilgrimage. On Christmas Day, massive numbers of anchovies appeared in the waters off the tiny seaside city of White Rock on Semiahmoo Bay, the southeastern portion of Boundary Bay. In my post-holiday indolence, I did not hear about their arrival until several days later and did not bestir myself to investigate until the afternoon of New Year's Eve.

Standing on the White Rock pier, it seemed everything around me was in motion. At least 200 people were strolling on the pier and paved walkways on the shore. The air over the water was filled with gulls wheeling, screaming, diving into the water and bobbing up again amid more gulls and ducks—Buffleheads, Goldeneye, and Surf Scoters—my spouse refused to let me name my orange plastic kayak "Surf Scoter" despite its resemblance to the duck's broad sloping bill; she said it sounded too much like scrotum—paddling frantically in mixed flocks on the surface. Perhaps 20 California Sea Lions in flotillas of six or eight patrolled back and forth, sweeping the water with open mouths and rearing up to bark at each other. The Harbor Seals were doing their best to avoid territory disputes by keeping their profiles low. On the shore, Northwestern Crows and gulls of several species picked through the dead fish, tossing the less choice aside.

Looking down from the pier, the place where my shadow fell on the water was green and at first seemed opaque. Then my perspective shifted and a flash of silver revealed that what looked like tiny brushstrokes on the green, slight darkenings of the water were actually thousands of finger-length fish, torpedo-shaped and very thin. Some were only a body's width apart and others more widely dispersed—perhaps a body's length. But the mass of them extended deeper and farther into the water than my eyes could distinguish, and I was reminded again of Jeff the river diver's observations about surface and depth and God.

Anchovies are a "pelagic forage fish," meaning that they live closer to the surface than the bottom of the ocean and that they are eaten by larger fish, mammals, and invertebrates like octopus and squid. They are a food source vital to the breeding success of some seabirds and make up over 90 percent of the diets of Chinook Salmon and California Sea Lions, at different times of the year. Anchovies themselves are low on the food chain, primary consumers that eat plankton and recently hatched fish. Other pelagic foragers include sardines and herring.

Taxonomically, anchovies are a family that includes over 100 species, which typically live in temperate waters. Anchovies are a significant food-fish for humans, often preserved dried as a soup base in parts of Asia and salt-preserved as a condiment in Europe. These techniques resemble first century Near Eastern preservation of another forage fish. On the Sea of Galilee, Kinneret Sardines were salted and preserved in the town of Magdala, for whom the famous biblical Mary, first witness to Jesus' resurrection, was named. Kinneret Sardines are also considered a likely candidate for the "two small fish" in the feeding of the 5,000. In the Gospels, fish stories are often concerned with the food security of small communities on the one hand, and the economic extraction systems of empires on the other.

The White Rock anchovies are part of the northern sub-population of Northern (or California) Anchovy, which live off of the West Coast of this continent. We are near the northern end of their range, but anchovies have become increasingly common in British Columbia waters in the past five years, due to warmer ocean temperatures. Northern Anchovies are fished commercially; a small proportion goes to human consumption, but the majority are used as feed for industrially raised livestock and farmed fish.

The abundance of pelagic forage fish can fluctuate dramatically. Andrew Trites, of the University of British Columbia's Institute for the Oceans and Fisheries, speculated that the fish in White Rock were driven to the surface and then to shore by whales and other marine mammals, and that they were dying in great numbers because there was simply not enough oxygen in the water to sustain them. Marine scientists in California warn that anchovy populations as well as those of other forage fish have declined sharply in their usual offshore habitat, due to rising ocean temperatures and overfishing, and that their congregating near shore signifies a population in distress. Scientists who have studied Northern Anchovies say that their increase is correlated with rises in ocean temperature and that their continued presence may impact species dynamics in the Salish Sea.

Walking on the beach above the band of dead fish on the shore, I startled a mixed flock of gulls, a few Ring-billed Gulls with yellow legs, black wing-tips, round heads and a dark ring on their bills, but mostly immature Glaucous-winged Gulls. To me these are the quintessential gull, meaning probably that they are the kind I most often see: a large gull with pink feet, a bright white head and light grey wings. Juveniles are mottled grey brown all over. Used to begging, scavenging, and outright stealing fish and chips off of tourists, the gulls were much more tolerant of humans than the geese had been, but a flock erupted gloriously all around me, and as my vision was obscured by grey wings I had a linguistic aha! moment. Glaucous, glaucoma—glaucous means grey!

Continuing to think about names and their meanings, should this inundation of anchovies be called a *school*, a *shoal*, or something else? Dame Juliana's *Boke of Seynt Albans* does not give any company terms for fish. In *The Compleat Angler*, Juliana's 17ᵗʰ century successor, Izaak Walton, uses the collectives *skulls* (schools) and shoals interchangeably, as most of us do, but in modern ichthyology and mathematical modeling, the two words have different meanings.

A quick "fun with words" detour into Greek: *Ichthys* is the Greek word for fish; it is also the proper name of that Jesus-fish image (derived from a first century acronym) that some Christians like to slap on their car bumpers like rainbow flags. *Theo* means god, *Ornis* bird. *Logia*, from the Greek for word, has come to mean study or discipline. So the study of fish, birds and religion are: ichthyology, ornithology, and theology respectively. Ted Lyddon Hatten, a pastor-turned-artist whose work often features birds, sometimes refers to his work as "ornith-theology" a term that I like to borrow for writing like this, about birds and big questions. During the writing phase of this project, my delight in creation sometimes took the form of fascination with the grotesque or risqué: exploding caterpillars, gay bat sex, the colonization history of bird poop, and this blanket of rotting fish. I like to think of these musings, which are really an avenue of wonder at the world, as "ick"-theology.

But, back to schooling and shoaling. A shoal is a group of fish, sometimes of different species, that aggregates socially. A school is a group of fish, almost always of the same species, moving in a synchronous and coordinated fashion at the same speed in a common direction. A school of fish is analogous to a murmuration of birds, and individuals within the group employ the same tactics—tracking and adjusting to a few individuals ahead and to the sides—to coordinate their movements. So the Northern Anchovies in White Rock were a shoal, which, in avoiding predators, may have schooled on their way to the pier. Salmon fry and adult salmon returning to spawn sometimes shoal, but anchovies are "obligate shoalers"; they live their whole lives in the company of others of their kind. Shoaling has several advantages. It creates a shared predator-detection system, increases the likelihood that your neighbour will be eaten instead of you, and makes foraging more successful. Travel with a pool of potential mates also makes it easier to find those proverbial "other fish in the sea."

With so many of this shoal dead on the shore on the last day of the year, I thought again about our time as an age of extinction. In May of 2019, when the Great Blue Herons were feeding their chicks, the United Nations released its Global Assessment Report on Biodiversity. Compiled over three years by experts from more than 50 nations, it reported that life on Earth is declining at rates unprecedented in human history with one million plant and animal species threatened with extinction within decades and one in four vulnerable. The report stated that humans are eroding the foundations of our own livelihood and called for "transformative change." In December the federal government of Canada promised to transition from salmon farms (where Atlantic Salmon in pens are fed Northern Anchovies and endanger wild Pacific Salmon) to closed-containment systems by 2025. I fear these changes are not sufficiently transformative.

Sobered, I looked out across the sand and water at hundreds of thousands of tiny fish. I did not feel a sense of affinity, but I was awed. Except perhaps for the moths, this was largest gathering of creatures I had experienced in my year of big numbers, and I was overwhelmed by their abundance, spread out in three dimensions. In the lunar calendar of the Heiltsuk people, who live on the central coast of British Columbia, the milky-appearing moon in February is said to be filled up with another forage fish, Pacific Herring. In March, when the moon appears as an inverted bowl, it is said to have tipped over, releasing fish into the sea. While these were not herring, it felt like the waters held an entire moon-full of tiny fish.

I headed home, ready to ring in the new year with my family and return to the Salmon Ceremony on the Chilliwack River in the morning.

SOURCES AND RESOURCES

The Compleat Angler

By Izaak Walton
Marriot, 1653
First published in 1653 and compiled from multiple sources, including Dame Juliana's *St. Albans*, this celebration of fishing includes technique, conservation, lifestyle, and humor. The book has been in almost continuous print for nearly 500 years and is available in forms from antique to e-book.

"Feeding Frenzy: Thousands of Fish Wash Up at White Rock Pier"

By Luisa Alvarez
CTV News Vancouver, December 26, 2019
A brief news account of the Northern Anchovies in White Rock, including an interview with a local marine scientist.

**"Feeding Frenzy: West Coast Anchovy Boom
Masks Ecosystem in Peril"**

By Alastair Bland
The New Humanitarian, September 28, 2017
A news article about anchovy abundance off the coast of California is published in Oceans Deeply, a digital media project on ocean health

**"Historical fluctuations and recent observations of
Northern Anchovy *Engraulis mordax* in the Salish Sea"**

By Willian Duguid, Jennifer Boldt et al.
Deep Sea Research Part II: Topical Studies in Oceanography, vol. 159, January 2019, pp. 22-41.
This scholarly article in a peer-reviewed journal suggests that the high incidence of Northern Anchovies in the Salish Sea is related to rising ocean temperatures, and that with continuing temperature change they may disrupt the balance of the local ecology.

Little Fish Big Impact: Managing a Crucial Link in Ocean Food Webs

By E. Pikitch, P.D. Boersma et al.

Lenfest Ocean Program, 2012
This is an extensive, well-illustrated report published by a global scientific taskforce on forage fish. It documents the vulnerability of forge fish to overfishing and population collapse and makes recommendations to reduce harvests.

Swimmy

By Leo Lionni
Knopf, 1963
This beautifully illustrated and award winning picture book about a smart and courageous little fish uses schooling and shoaling behaviour as a metaphor for collective action.

GLOSSARY

Accipiter
A diverse genus of long-tailed, raptors with short, rounded wings, also called true hawks.

Albumen
The clear part of an egg that surrounds the yolk and supplies the developing embryo with water and protein, also called the white.

Alevin
Newly hatched salmonid still attached to the yolk sac.

Allopreening
A behavior in birds where one individual positions and cleans the feathers of another, usually on the head and neck.

Alluvial
Describes a geologically young deposit made up of clay, slit, sand, or gravel left by running water.

Altricial
Refers to young of a species that are born or hatched in an immature state requiring feeding and care. The opposite of precocial.

Amplexus
A type of mating behavior in which a male grasps a female with his front legs and fertilizes the eggs, after they are released from the female's body.

Anadromous
Describes fish which are born in freshwater, spend most of their lives in saltwater and migrate up rivers from the sea to spawn.

Anthropocene
Proposed name for the current geological epoch characterized by human impact on climate and species.

Benthic
Describes the bottom of lakes or oceans, the adjacent water and organisms that live there.

Blue List
The group of species and ecosystems with conservation status ranks that give cause for special concern; species and ecosystems considered vulnerable in a particular location.

Breeding Population
The number of sexually mature individuals within a group presumed to be engaging in reproductive activity.

Carrying Capacity
The maximum population of a particular organism that can be sustained indefinitely by the resources in a particular environment without depleting those resources.

Casting
A ball of indigestible fur, feathers, bones and other matter regurgitated by a raptor. The best known are owl pellets. Casting can also refer to the act of expelling the material as in "casting a pellet."

Citizen Science
The participation of members of the public in scientific research, often by collecting biological and conservation data in local areas that they know well.

Cloaca
A common outlet into which intestinal, urinary and genital tracts open, found in birds, amphibians, reptiles, monotremes, and some fish.

Defaunation
The phenomenon of global, local, or functional extinction of wild animal species and mass depletion of their numbers.

Detritivore
An organism that feeds on dead and decaying plant and animal matter.

Diurnal
Active during the day, opposite of nocturnal.

Dorsal
From the Latin for back, refers to the back or upper side of an organism, opposite of ventral.

Eft
The gill-less terrestrial juvenile phase of some newts and salamanders. An adaptation that allows an otherwise aquatic species to disperse over land to locate new aquatic habitats.

Entomology
The branch of zoology that is the scientific study of insects.

Eremocene
The age of loneliness, a term introduced by biologist E.O. Wilson, for the current era to draw attention to the loss of species and individuals.

Estuary
The transition zone between river and ocean, the tidal mouth of a river or stream

Etymology
The study of the origin of words and their development over time.

Extirpated
Locally extinct, no longer existing in a particular area.

Falcon
Raptors of the genus Falco, fast fliers with long pointed wings.

Frass
The solid excrement of insects and their larvae.

Freshet
The annual high water or flooding of a river caused by spring thaw.

Fry
Immature salmonids that have absorbed their yolk sac, use a swim bladder, and live in fresh water.

Functional Extinction
When a species has been so reduced in numbers that it no longer plays any significant role in its ecosystem.

Guano
Seabird and bat excrement used as plant fertilizer because of its high nitrogen, phosphate, and potassium content.

Hatch year
A bird which hatched during the current calendar year.

Hibernacula
Shelters occupied in winter by dormant animals. (singular hibernaculum)

Instar
The developmental life phase between moulting of an insect or other invertebrate.

Kype
The upturned hook that develops on the lower jaw of some male salmonids at sexual maturity.

Lexicographer
A linguist who specializes in the inventory of words in a particular language. The author or editor of a dictionary.

Life List
A birder's cumulative record of all the bird species sighted in the wild and identified with certainty during their lifetime.

Lore
The area between the eyes and nostrils of a bird, reptile, or amphibian.

Murmuration
A large group of small birds flocking together in coordinated motion, with frequent changes of direction.

Ornithophobia
Fear of birds.

Otolith
Calcium carbonate "ear stones" found in the inner ear of vertebrates used in balance and spatial orientation.

Oviduct
The tube through which an egg passes from ovary to the site of fertilization.

Pelagic
The column of water in oceans and lakes that is neither near the bottom nor the shore. Can also refer to organisms that live there, particularly in the open sea.

Phototaxis
Movement of an organism toward or away from a stimulus of light.

Pollinator
An organism that is a vector in the sexual reproduction of plants, moving pollen from the male anther of one flower to the female stigma of another flower.

Polygyny
A form of polygamy in which a male mates with more than one female.

Precocial
Refers to young of a species that are born or hatched in a relatively mature state able to move and feed almost immediately. The opposite of altricial.

Red List
The group of species and ecosystems whose conservation status is most at risk of endangerment, extinction, or extirpation.

Redd
A shallow nest dug in gravel by a fish in which eggs are deposited.

Retrices
The large, stiff feathers in a bird's tail used for steering in flight. (singular retrix)

Salish Sea
The marine ecosystem that includes the straits, sounds, channels and waterways between the Olympic Peninsula, Vancouver Island and the mainland of British Columbia and Washington State.

Salmonid
Member of the family Salmonidae, elongate bony fishes including salmon and trout.

School
A group of fish, almost always of the same species, moving in a synchronous and coordinated fashion at the same speed in a common direction.

Sedge
A large family of grass-like flowering plants with triangular stems. Rarely, a collective noun for herons and bitterns.

Semelparous
Describes the reproductive strategy where individuals have a single reproductive episode before death.

Sexual Dimorphism
Where there is significant size or external appearance difference between sexes.

Shifting Baseline Syndrome
The gradual change in accepted norms, usually declining size, abundance, or diversity in ecosystems, whereby each new generation assumes the situation in which they were raised is normal.

Shoal
A group of fish, sometimes of different species, that aggregates socially.

Smolt
A young salmonid that has developed a silvery colour and is physiologically ready for life in the ocean.

Spicule
A small sharp, needle-like anatomical structure.

Splay
White splatter caused by the liquid excretion of large birds.

Spraint
Otter feces.

Trophic
Refers to feeding or energy source relationships within a nutritional system.

Ventral
Refers to the front or lower side of an organism, opposite of dorsal.

Windshield Phenomenon
Fewer dead insects accumulate on car windshields than in previous decades. This is a place where is the global decline in insect populations is often observed.

RELATED TITLES BY HANCOCK HOUSE

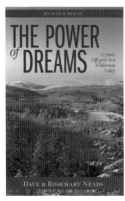

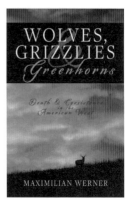
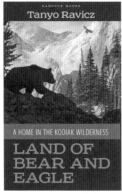